50 AWESOME HOME BUSINESSES BELOW $500 & EZ START-UP GUIDE©

By: Helena Schaar

Live
The Life of Your Dreams!
Achieve Ultimate Freedom & Success!
Find the Perfect Work At Home Job for You!
Begin Now With Less Than $500 in Start-up Costs!
Make a Good Income, Set Your Own Hours & Have More Free Time!
Enjoy Success in Life & Work, & Love Your Job. Be an Entrepreneur!

This book tells you absolutely everything you need to know to start and run a successful home-based business. Includes the very best and most successful income earning home businesses that you can begin right now with minimal start up costs. Many new, unique, and fantastic business ideas are included. Provides an in-depth study of the 20 very best home businesses, plus a list of 30 more excellent home business ideas. These are also the top choices for being quick and simple to get started within four months or less, and many can be started immediately. Includes the details, facts, secrets, and inside scoop from experts currently successful in these home businesses. Everyone can find the perfect home business inside this book. This is also the ultimate "how to" guide to quickly and easily get a business up and running profitably.

Inside find important information about how to choose the best home business for you. How to start up any type of home-based business, how to successfully operate the business, how to design your contracts and manuals, how to price your services, how much money you can make, finding free and low cost advertising, and how to do your own taxes. There is also information about the best way to get a wealth of information specific to your geographic area. The EZ start-up guide will help you minimize the red tape, and get your business up and running properly in record time.

1

50 AWESOME HOME BUSINESSES
BELOW $500
& EZ START-UP GUIDE©

About the author:

Helena Schaar is a professional licensed healthcare therapist, college faculty member, and writer. Publications to date include over 30 articles and books. These writings are designed to inspire, motivate, and promote optimal personal and financial health, wealth, and success.

Helena and her family live happily in the sunshine state of Florida. Helena is a lifelong devotee health, fitness, and living a positive, joyful, Christian life. Having plenty of quality family time is a top priority.

This book is dedicated to my son, Jasen, whom I love with all my heart and soul.

TABLE OF CONTENTS

Topic   **Page Number**

<u>INTRODUCTION</u>

Live
The Life of Your Dreams!
Achieve Ultimate Freedom & Success!
Find the Perfect Work At Home Job for You!
Begin Now With Less Than $500 in Start-up Costs!
Make a Good Income, Set Your Own Hours & Have More Free Time!
Enjoy Success in Life & Work, & Love Your Job. Be an Entrepreneur!

This book tells you absolutely everything you need to know to start and run a successful home-based business. Includes the very best and most successful income earning home businesses that you can begin right now with minimal start up costs. Many new, unique, and fantastic business ideas are included. Provides an in-depth study of the 20 very best home businesses, plus a list of 30 more excellent home business ideas. These are also the top choices for being quick and simple to get started within four months or less, and many can be started immediately. Includes the details, facts, secrets, and inside scoop from experts currently successful in these home businesses. Everyone can find the perfect home business inside this book. This is also the ultimate "how to" guide to quickly and easily get a business up and running profitably.

Inside find important information about how to choose the best home business for you. How to start up any type of home-based business, how to successfully operate the business, how to design your contracts and manuals, how to price your services, how much money you can make, finding free and low cost advertising, and how to do your own taxes. There is also information about the best way to get a wealth of information specific to your geographic area. The EZ start-up guide will help you minimize the red tape, and get your business up and running properly in record time.

There is a home business opportunity for everyone. All have had some life experience, a favorite hobby, special skills, natural talents, or an idea of something you always wanted to do. This makes the basis for your home business. Everyone can find something they enjoy in these home business ideas, match it to their own skills and talents, and turn it into a successful business. That's what it's all about. Finding a career you love so you can enjoy your life more!

This book is not about get rich quick ideas. These are successful, proven, practical, income-producing businesses. You <u>do</u> have to be motivated to put in the time, effort, and work in order to succeed and become prosperous in your home business.

Another great benefit of owning a home business is that you will save lots of time and money by working from home. The 10 second commute time to your home office or home workspace saves you about one hour travel time per day and saves you on gas and car expenses. Also you can work anytime you want, a couple hours in the morning, a few hours in the evening, or a straight eight hours if you so choose.

Carefully compare the amount of income from a home business versus that of a regular job. You can make more money than it appears at first glance when running a home business. This extra income comes in the form of saved money, or money returned to you when you file your taxes due to:
- Home business expenses
- Home office expenses
- Home office depreciation
- Supplies, equipment, furniture used in the business - deductible & depreciable
- Car and travel expenses (or money saved if you do not travel at all)
- And much more as you can see in the tax section.

These are all allowable, legitimate, and legal tax deductions. Our government wants the small business owner to succeed, and gives many tax incentives to small business owners. This is all explained further in the tax guide section.

Once you figure in the advantages of the tax deductions, plus the wonderful benefits like being your own boss, making your own schedule, lowering your stress, getting lot's more free time, and the personal sense of satisfaction and accomplishment at owning your own business............it is well worth it!

If you choose a business that is home-based, with much of the work done outside your home, you are still classified as a home business owner, and still get to enjoy the tax benefits including deductions and depreciation allowances for your home office, supplies, equipment, furniture, and your car. This applies as long as your business home base is your home, and you are running the business from your home. In all of the home-based businesses in this book, you will be conducting some business activity in your home office or home workspace. You will need to perform paperwork, bookkeeping, record keeping, billing, calling clients, or conducting some such business activity from your home. Your home office may be an office inside your home, or simply a workspace with a table and chair used for business with some office supplies and a file cabinet. The larger your business workspace, the larger your home business deductions because deductions and depreciation are based partly on the percentage of the home you are using for the business. See the tax guide section to get more information on exactly which tax books you need. These tax books are free, and available from the IRS.

Also, if you choose one of the businesses where you travel to client's homes, you get the added benefit of the car expense reimbursement when you do your taxes. For example, if you travel to two clients homes one day, for a total of 50 miles, you will receive an additional $18.50 back on your taxes for that one day as car expense reimbursement (sample at 37 cents per mile, see the tax guide section).

One home business expert, a computer programmer making $35 per hour started a home cleaning business because she did not want to continue the full time Monday to Friday 8 to 5 hours while her children were young. She wanted to try her own business until the youngest child entered first grade, and then return to her lucrative computer programming job. The only other thing she knew a lot about was cleaning the house, and it was something she loved to do. She always had the cleanest house on the block. She also likes the idea of an active job with the benefit of getting some exercise on the job instead of sitting at a desk all day. For her it was a major change. So with this love of cleaning and motivation to set her own part time schedule, and the desire to have more time with her family, she launched a home cleaning business. The demand for this business is huge and she soon had so many clients, she had to hire 3 others to work with her. She then earned a percentage of their wages as supervisor of these independent contractors. She now works an average 25 hours per week, making more than her previous full time job. She loves her schedule and her business, and has lots of time to be with her family. She also lost 15 pounds on the way with all the physical activity. At this point it is safe to say she will most likely not return to the full time job she previously had.

Choosing The Best Home Business for You

Finding the best home business for you is all about figuring out what you love to do, or finding something new that peaks your interest, and turning it into an income-producing business. There is a perfect home business opportunity for everyone. All have had some life experience, work experience, a favorite hobby, special skills, or natural talents. You may also have something in mind that you have always wanted to do, or you may discover something new in this book that looks like an interesting job opportunity. Find something you enjoy, that satisfies your personal expectations of a great job, and that is the perfect business for you.

Read over the list of 50 businesses, and the top 20 job descriptions. Write down four or five ideas that look the best to you. The detailed descriptions include general information about the business, personal characteristics to match you to a business, necessary skills and knowledge, average earnings, start-up costs, how to get started, and helpful resources. There is also a guide for "Important Aspects to Consider in a Home Business". This guide will help you get complete and comprehensive information on the internet for any of the 50 businesses. Assessing this data will help you evaluate your choices, and narrow them down. Be sure to read about getting information that is specific to your geographic area, so you can find out exactly what you can expect to earn, and find out how much competition you have. With all of this information, you will be able to narrow down your list, and choose the best business for you to start.

Some home business owners run two or three of these businesses simultaneously, with each providing a small to moderate amount of income. Why would someone want more than one business? It is not much different than being a freelance person who has multiple income sources from several different clients. A home business owner may have a seasonal business, or they may have a business they love, but not make quite enough income to live on, so they start a second business. Some even have three businesses, love the variety of the work they do, and would not have it any other way. If you find several businesses that look great, make a list of these for future reference. It is best to fully concentrate on starting one business at a time. Your business should be completely mastered so you can perform it with skill, efficiency, and complete confidence and competence. After you have mastered the business, you may consider adding a second business.

Some examples of entrepreneurs with more than one business follow:

One of the home business experts has a babysitting service and provides care for one child in addition to one of her own. This provides her with a nice little extra income source, and gives her child a fun playmate. This also gives her occasional breaks from entertaining her only child all the time, because the two children play happily together and entertain each other under her supervision at least one or two hours each day.

She knits and crochets a few hours per week when the children are happily playing together. This is a hobby she has had since childhood. These beautiful crafts are sold on eBay as fast as she can make them.

So she has 3 jobs providing regular income streams, and loves them all. (Childcare, crafts, and selling on eBay). She would not be happy to have a full-fledged in-home daycare because she does not feel she has the desire or the skills needed to care for 4 to 8 children, (although many enjoy the in-home daycare, it is just not for her). She also feels it may be too sedentary to sit and knit 40 hours per week. Therefore having 3 jobs works best for her, and provides a great income sufficient to live on.

Another home business owner has the following three businesses:

She is a landlord, owning one rental property providing good income. She purchased this with less than $400 down, and chose a condo so there would be no outside maintenance worries.

She provides tax preparation services to other small business owners, concentrating on landlords with rental property. This was easy once she learned how to do her own record keeping and taxes. The rental property and tax preparation only keep her busy at tax time, plus one or two hours per week year round.

With all that spare time, she turned to her computer hobby of digital picture graphic design. She was an expert at taking pictures and turning them into beautiful greeting cards, calendars, albums, and more. She turned this hobby into a business of designing book covers for writers. With an internet home page as her only advertisement, internet search engines lead plenty of business her way.

All together, she works 20 – 35 hours per week, sets her own schedule, makes a great income, and is very happy. She enjoys the variety of her work and would not have it any other way.

IMPORTANT ASPECTS TO CONSIDER IN A HOME BUSINESS

These are the important points to consider, and important questions to ask, for any type of home business you have an interest in starting.

DESCRIPTION OF THE BUSINESS:

An overview and general description of the home business. The general day to day operation of the home business. Is the daily activity involved in the business something that you would enjoy? Does the business involve travel, or is all the work done at home? Will you be able to set your own schedule? How much competition is there?

MATCHING PERSONAL CHARACTERISTICS:

Determine if your personality characteristics are right for this type of work. What personal traits work best with this business? Decide if you would like a business dealing with lots of people, or you prefer to work independently in your home office. Do you enjoy speaking in front of a group? Do you enjoy senior citizens? Do you enjoy computer work and paperwork? Also, decide if you would enjoy some travel time in your business or not, and how much travel would be involved in the business you choose. Use your answers to match yourself to the best business for you.

NECESSARY SKILLS & KNOWLEDGE:

Identify the special skills, talents, life experience, and work experience you already possess. Then think about anything you have always wanted to do, or learn more about. Most ideas in this book are either those skills possessed by certain people, or new skills that can be learned within a few months.

AVERAGE EARNINGS:

How much do you expect to earn in your home business? The average hourly earnings vary based on your geographic area of the country. You can expect to earn more if you live in a large city, or in a geographic area where the cost of living and income levels are significantly higher than the national average. You may earn less if you live in a geographic area where the income levels and cost of living are significantly less than the national average. It is best to check with local competitors to get the best income estimates.

START-UP COSTS:

How much will it cost to begin the home business? Every business in this book can be started for under $500. It is assumed you have a computer, printer, and internet access, since most households do. If you do not have these essentials, you can still start one of these businesses for under $500. You would need to either purchase a used computer and printer, or access them free at places like the public library.

Internet access is readily available from a many companies with a price range suitable to everyone. There are also free internet providers, however, your time on the internet may be limited, and connections may be slower and not as readily available as paid access providers. There is also free internet access available at public libraries. If you access these at the library, you will need to find the best time to go that will allow you to use them for an extended period of time. Many libraries have a time limit of 30 minutes or so for computers with internet access when there are others waiting to use the computers. For some of these businesses, you may need specific software programs. These are readily available at office supply stores. Some very good software is even free on the internet, search for "free software".

Also review the section "Starting Your Home Business" for key components needed in almost every home businesses. Remember that all costs associated with your business are tax deductible expenses, or eligible for depreciation allowances.

RESOURCES - INTERNET SEARCH ENGINE KEY WORDS:

With the internet, it is so easy to find the most current resources and those resources specific to your geographic area. Having a list of names and phone numbers that will soon be outdated, or useless out of your geographic area, is not as worthwhile as up-to-the-minute resources on the internet. Recommended search engines are Google, MSN, and Yahoo, among others. To find a wealth of resources on the internet, type in the important keywords such as the business name, or business type, or any important key words about starting the business. Next, add your city & state to the search. This way you can get the best information for your geographic area. Example " business license + (your state/city)".

Starting Your Home Business

The most important components of beginning a home-based business are listed here. Each is listed with details in this section:

- **Naming the business**

- **Obtaining the business license**

- **Obtaining a zoning permit, if required**

- **Insurance and bonding, if required**

- **Designing your contracts**

- **Pricing your products and services**

- **Advertising your business**

Business License and Business Name

Once you decide on the business you want to start, you will need to choose a name for the business. Some like to put an exact name on the business like "Jack's Lawn Care" while others choose something that does not limit your services, in case you decide to get 2 businesses going or change businesses. With a good choice of a name, you may be able to keep one name for several businesses. One example is "Superior Services". You can then add to the name as you choose, such as "Superior Resume Services", or "Superior Computer Training Services".

Next you need to check with your state, county, and city to see what is required by law in order to operate the home business. It is very important to find out if zoning laws and other laws allow you to operate the business from your home. You also need to check for any rules, regulations, and bylaws with your homeowners association, or landlord, if applicable to you.

Important business matters:

- <u>Fictitious Name Registration</u> - Most states require some type of application be filed to give your business a name. This is quick and easy to do, and is available on line in some states. This costs approximately $50, and is good for 5 years in some states. ($10/Year)

- <u>Zoning Permit</u> - Some states, cities, or counties require that you obtain a zoning permit to operate your business out of your home, while others do not. The cost ranges from about $10 to $50, and is usually a one-time fee.

- <u>Business License</u> - (Also called an occupational license or business permit). This ranges from about $30 to $80 per year.

- <u>Insurance & Bonding</u> - You should check into getting insurance and bonding to protect you and your business. (First check and see if your homeowners insurance covers you before you purchase an additional insurance plan). If everyone in your chosen field advertises they are " Licensed, Bonded, and Insured", chances are you need the same in order to be in business. The cost of insurance and bonding varies greatly depending on the business, with an average of $15 per month for most businesses listed in this book.

- <u>Miscellaneous Yearly Requirements</u> - Depending on the business you choose, you need to find out about any other miscellaneous yearly requirements. There may be a few hours of required educational classes, and/or some type of licensure renewal requirements.

Purchasing your own health insurance is completely up to each individual. You may want to consider purchasing health insurance if you are not covered by your spouse, or by other means. There is affordable health insurance available for healthy individuals, and can be easily found on an internet search. Search for "individual health insurance". Health insurance costs may be 100% deductible on your taxes. There are also health care plans, dental care plans, and vision care plans available to individuals and small business owners.

Designing Your Contracts

Do some research on the internet and at local businesses of the same type you are considering to start. Find out what services and products they have to offer, and the average pricing of these products and services in your geographic area. Closely review the information you obtain from two or three of those you consider the best competitive businesses. Use this information as a reference to help you formulate your own business plan, contracts, pricing, and list of services. Be sure your are only using the information you obtain as a reference. Never copy other people's documents to use as your own, as the documents are protected by copyright laws.

You can find sample forms, contracts, manuals, and general information about competitive businesses easily on the internet. Rarely, business owners may actually say you are welcome to use all of their forms and contracts in your business. Examples we found include a few very generous home daycare providers with forms on the internet, and notices that state you can use their forms for your own home business. It is always best to print a copy of these permissions to use material.

Pricing Your Products and Services

When you work on pricing your products or services, here again, do some research on the internet and at local businesses of the same type of business you are pursuing. Find out what others are charging for the same business products and/or services in your geographic area. You can then set a competitive price. Pricing a small percentage below the competition almost guarantees you some business. You can also advertise that you will beat any other price, which is a great success strategy for a new businesses. You can always raise your prices in the future, after your business is successful and you have built a good reputation.

Advertising Your Business

Advertising your business can take many directions. There are many free and low cost advertising methods. It is a good idea to have business cards and stationary with your business name. You can pass out your business cards anytime and anywhere.

Free or nearly free advertising methods are quite numerous. Always verify first that it is allowed to advertise by your selected method. Free and nearly free advertising includes placing signs where allowed, placing informational fliers on bulletin boards at local grocery stores, laundromats, colleges, and other local businesses that allow ads. Also you can advertise in newsletters (some of which are free) including churches, local hospitals, senior citizen groups, or other target age groups with newsletters. Another method is placing your fliers on car windshields at places with plenty of cars like grocery stores, variety stores, shopping malls, or strip-malls.

Low cost advertising includes placing an ad in your local newspaper or community newspaper. Also target age specific or group specific community newspapers, brochures, and newsletters if appropriate for your business. Examples: The Parent/Child Connection, The Senior Citizens Monthly Newsletter. Some internet websites allow you to post a free ad, but you will pay a small fee for most internet advertising. Once you are up and running, you can consider getting your own website to promote your product or services. There are many low cost websites easily found with a simple internet search. If you plan to sell on the internet, be sure to check the fees for accepting charge cards and personal checks. These fees can vary greatly, so compare carefully. Some web hosting services do not provide services for accepting payments at all, so do some research before deciding what is best for you and your business.

Additional Information about Starting a Business:

Setting goals, remaining motivated, and having a positive attitude will go a long way in assuring your business succeeds. You also need plenty of enthusiasm and perseverance. Always remember there are millions of people who are already living their dream with their own home business, and making a good income, and so can do it to.

In all your business dealings, present a courteous professional manner. It is important to be positive, cheerful, enthusiastic, and businesslike with all of your business contacts. You also need to be serious about your business if you want others to take you seriously.

Be sure to visit the U.S. Small Business Administration (SBA) website at www.sba.gov. The SBA gives you a wealth of information about small business start-up, operation, financing, and leads you to more resources. You should not need financing to begin any of the businesses listed in this book. However, if you choose to expand, or just want to know what help is available to you, the SBA is an excellent resource.

Here are a few motivational quotes and inspirational favorites
 of successful home business owners:

Goals are dreams we formulate into plans, and take actions to fulfill.

Accomplishments can be measured by the obstacles overcome to reach the goals.

Giving your best effort makes you the winner.

Success occurs when opportunity meets preparation.

Success is made up of a series of little daily efforts.

In order to succeed, you must know, like, and believe in what you are doing.

Success is connected to action. Successful people keep moving, overcome obstacles, and never quit.

Hard work is the foundation of all business, the source of all prosperity, and the parent of genius.

The foundation for balanced success consists of faith, integrity, honesty, character and hard work.

The top 20 home businesses are listed in this guide with complete details. They are not in order of the best, as they are all good businesses for somebody, and are all proven successful home-based businesses. The next 30 excellent home business ideas are then listed. All of these can be up and running within a few months, and all cost less than $500 to start. These are all real income-producing businesses millions of people are currently operating profitably!

50 AWESOME HOME BUSINESSES

1. Family Home Daycare or Nanny/Babysitting Service

2. Elder Care Service

3. Errand/Courier Service

4. Mobile Notary Public &/or Professional Signing Agent

5. Ebay - Buying and Selling

6. Ebay - Make and Sell Anything

7. Gift Basket Business

8. CPR-BLS Instructor

9. First Aid Instructor

10. Personal Fitness Trainer

11. Computer Tutor

12. Wedding Consultant - Planner

13. Reunion Planner - Organizer

14. Secretarial Service

15. Resume Writing Service

16. Tax Preparation Service

17. Sell Health Care Plans and/or Dental Care Plans

18. Pet Sitting Service, Pet Boarding, Pet Transportation

19. Residential Cleaning Service

20. Pool Cleaning & Maintenance Service

21. Teach Beginning Music Lessons

22. Sell Child ID Kits

23. Sell Prepaid Legal Plans

24. Distributor for Diet/Weight Loss Products

25. Distributor for Anti-Wrinkle, Anti-Aging Products

26. Sell Beauty Products Like Avon or Mary Kay

27. Specialty Cake Making/Decorating - Birthdays, weddings, and other special occasions

28. Entertainer for Children's Birthday Parties Magician, Clown, Face Painting

29. Party & Event Planner

30. Tour Organizer

31. Party Rentals (Kids inflatable bouncers, misc party supplies)

32. Tutor for School-Age Children

33. Substitute Homeschool Teacher

33. Book Cover Designer for Writers

34. Professional Answering Service

35. Business Plan Writer

36. Court Reporters Assistant Typist (Note Reader/Scopist)

37. Bookkeeper for Home-Based Businesses

38. Video Tape Duplication Service

39. Professional Organizer

40. Freelance Writer

41. Book Cover Designer for Writers

42. Proofreading/Editing/Indexing Service for Writers

43. Indoor Environmental Tester

44. Real Estate Landlord – Start with one property, low money down

45. Handyman – Home Repair Service

46. Lawn Care/Landscaping Business

47. Home Décor Specialist – Painting murals on walls or decorative wallpaper

48. Floor Cleaning Business - Specialize in Carpets or Hardwood Floors

49. Window Cleaning Service or Window Blind Cleaning Service

50. Automobile Detailing Business

THE TOP 20 HOME BUSINESSES

#1 Family Home Daycare or Nanny/Babysitting Service

DESCRIPTION OF THE BUSINESS:

In today's society the majority of women with children under six work either full-time or part-time. While some of these women have relatives or friends to care for their preschool children while they work, many need some type of childcare services. They seek high quality, caring, nurturing, educational, reliable care for their children. Some working mothers use formal daycare centers or preschools while others prefer in-home family daycare, nanny, or babysitting services. As a family daycare provider you can provide more individualized care, and more attention to each child than daycare centers due to lower adult to child ratios. If you also offer to teach age-appropriate educational activities, the child can benefit greatly, and the parent may choose you over other in home daycares that only include play time, no educational activities.

NECESSARY SKILLS & KNOWLEDGE:

If you love children, you can get into this business. Prior experience is a plus, even experience with your own children, grandchildren, or any other babysitting jobs in the past. Most parents will ask for references.

To provide childcare for one or two children, there is not usually a state licensing requirement. Always check with your state laws to be sure you are in compliance. Most states require a license to operate an in-home daycare once you go above a certain number of children in your care. If you decide to open a licensed in home daycare, you must complete a state required educational program that is approximately 30 hours in length. This may be free, or there may be a small charge of up to $50. You will also have to have your home inspected for safety, and possibly a zoning permit. Once all the requirements have been met you are licensed as a family home daycare provider and can provide care for up to eight children depending on their age group and your state requirements. You should also check into insurance if you operate a daycare.

AVERAGE EARNINGS:

You can expect to earn more income with infants, and the income declines as the child gets older. Taking care of one infant full time, income is about $150 per week. Taking care of one 4-year old, the income is about $80 per week. With a licensed in home daycare, you can earn anywhere from $20,000 to $50,000 per year. You are also eligible for special benefits like food subsidies for the children to assure good nutrition. Your state licensing office has all the details.

START-UP COSTS:

Low start up costs at under $300. To be a babysitter or nanny caring for one or two children, there is usually no license needed, so start up costs will be under $100. Otherwise in-home daycare licensure including state-required classes costs under $100. You will need some age-appropriate toys and educational items. Parents usually supply the necessities like diapers and formula for infants, but this is negotiable between you and the parent.

****

#2 ELDER CARE

DESCRIPTION OF THE BUSINESS:

This is a business in very high demand, and lot's of opportunity for income for those choosing to pursue this career. The elderly who are no longer completely able to care for themselves need help. They may not need or want to live in a nursing home, so they usually live with some family members, and some live alone for as long as they are able to. They may need help with self-care and other activities of daily living. Some may want help with household tasks like cooking, laundry, tidying up. Their family or caregiver can not perform the tasks 100% of the time. Many of them want an occasional break from being a full time caregiver, and that is where the elder care business comes in.

Currently, most states do not have any special licensing requirement for those wishing to enter this business. To become a nursing assistant or home health aid you would need a license. As an elder care provider, you are not allowed to give medications or perform high-tech nursing duties, but you can help with personal care and hygiene including bathing, washing hair, and brushing teeth. Also care of the home, cleaning, changing bed linens, laundry, cooking a meal. Sometimes the full time caregiver just needs someone to sit with the elderly person while they leave the house. You may also provide elder care at your home. You then need to arrange transportation and have a suitable and comfortable room in your home for the elder in your care. Alternately, you can take care of handicapped persons.

This business is great for those who want the freedom of setting their own hours. You can decide how much income you want, as the demand greatly outpaces the supply of workers. Eventually you can even hire other people to perform the services, with you as the business owner and manager. You have to enjoy senior citizens. It helps if you have taken care of an elderly person, such as an aging relative by yourself. You must enjoy helping those who cannot help themselves.

NECESSARY SKILLS & KNOWLEDGE:

You must know how to perform the tasks that you advertise in your business. You may choose to only do a sitting service to watch the elder while the regular caregiver leaves. In that case, the only skills needed are a caring attitude and the ability to help the elder eat, drink or use the bathroom. You must know how to properly lift and transfer a person who may have limited mobility. This must be done using correct technique so that neither you nor the person you are caring for is injured. You must get information on each elder you care for regarding mobility limitations and special needs. If you advertise that you will cook, clean, do laundry, then those are necessary skills. Most people providing elder care services give assistance with personal hygiene such as bathing, washing hair, brushing teeth, changing clothes, and so forth.

If you have never taken care of an elderly person, you can learn the necessary skills. There are low cost and free classes at many community education centers and hospitals to instruct you in everything you need to know about taking care of elderly people. These courses are nursing assistant courses, or home health aid courses. The total hours to complete these are usually less than 30 hours. You could also learn by reading books from the library or finding information and even instructional videos at the library or on the internet. Performing correct transfers and lifting are especially important skills.

Next, you will need a simple manual and contract, especially for those who want to enlist your services on a regular basis, such as weekly. See the section titled "Designing Contracts and Manuals".

AVERAGE EARNINGS:

You can earn between $10 and $20 per hour on average, plus you will get tax deductions for use of the car and mileage. Experts in this business prefer to set a three hour minimum visit, and limit the driving to a 20 mile radius from home. You can call those who advertise elder care in your local newspaper to get a good idea of what they charge, and what they provide for the amount charged.

START-UP COSTS:

Super low start up costs at under $100. All you need is your vehicle and the desire and knowledge to provide care. One advertisement in the major local newspaper usually gets enough clientele to start the business.

****

#3 ERRAND/COURIER SERVICE

DESCRIPTION OF THE BUSINESS:

This is a home-based business with lots of travel involved. The majority of the work will be driving to and from homes and businesses. The best sources of business are mortgage companies and legal firms who use the services of couriers frequently to deliver important documents. Small businesses with few employees are also frequently in need of someone to perform an errand for them on short notice when they are unable to leave the business themselves. Other good sources of business involve high income individuals who hire and pay others to do many of their household tasks for them. Errands can be performed for any individual who does not wish to perform the errands themselves, those who do not have the time for errands, or those who do not have a vehicle for driving between errands.

Errand services can pick up and deliver documents, do the grocery shopping, take and pick up clothes from a laundromat, go to the post office, go to the mall to pick up a special gift, take items for return or exchange, deliver an item to a friends house, or any other errand imaginable.

Most errand/courier services do not provide transportation for children as this can pose liability issues. Some errand/courier services add pet transportation to their list of services, such as transporting pets to and from a veterinarian.

NECESSARY SKILLS & KNOWLEDGE:

You need good transportation and must be able to follow a map. To be happy in this business you have to enjoy driving. Many who choose this business like the idea of not being confined to an office. They enjoy getting outside, travelling around town, and doing lots of different things. It also helps to know your city very well, or be very good at following a map. This is much easier with internet access, as you can print an exact route to the destinations, and get estimated mileage and travel time.

You should be able to organize errands and tasks well, and be able to set a timetable. Some of your clients will need an errand done, or a delivery made by a certain time of the day, so you must be able to meet their expectations.

AVERAGE EARNINGS:

Average hourly rates range from $10 to $30 per hour. You have to figure in the amount of your travel time when giving estimates, as this time may be quite significant. Remember, your car and travel expenses are tax deductible or eligible for depreciation allowance, meaning you will be reimbursed for these travel expenses.

START-UP COSTS:

Very low at under $100 for anyone who already has good transportation. The initial expenses mostly involve advertising your business

****

#4 MOBILE NOTARY PUBLIC

DESCRIPTION OF THE BUSINESS:

People need the services of a notary public at various times throughout their lives with personal and business issues. With the popularity of using the internet to download forms and applications, notary services are needed more and more frequently because the people downloading these forms and applications are not presenting themselves to the place of business. Using a notary for mortgage loan documents is a very popular service. Some who pursue this business decide to take their career further by becoming a "Certified Signing Agent" (CSA). The CSA is needed frequently to go over mortgage loan documents with clients and notarize the documents. Offering mobile notary public services increases the income potential and is a good marketing tool since many people are filling out these documents in their homes. It is a major convenience to clients to complete the documents with notarization in the comfort of their homes. People also use notary public services for many other documents, many of which are legal documents. This includes: Wills, divorce documents, name change documents, adoption applications, and some employer required forms to name a few.

NECESSARY SKILLS & KNOWLEDGE:

You should enjoy working with people and be able to present a professional businesslike attitude. Excellent ability to pay close attention to details, plus good reading and comprehension skills are needed. Some experience with reading legal documents, mortgage documents, other loan applications, and other types of forms listed in the business description are helpful. Prior experience is good, but not necessary as long as you put in some time and effort reading and reviewing these types of forms to familiarize yourself with the business. (Many sample documents can be found on the internet). Some states require a one time educational course be completed to become a notary public. If required, it is available free or at minimal cost, available on the internet, and takes approximately three hours to complete. Reliable transportation for travelling to client's homes is a must in a mobile notary business.

AVERAGE EARNINGS:

You can expect to earn between $10 and $60 per notarization. The higher earnings are generally made by certified signing agents. One simple notarization can take as little as 10 minutes, and a complicated signing can take two to three hours.

START-UP COSTS:

Low start up costs at under $200 to become a notary public, under $300 to become a certified signing agent. The initial notary public designation plus bonding costs approximately $40, and is good for one year. Notary publics are always bonded. There are often specials with bonding companies that will give you bonding along with your notary designation for four years for $100 ($25 per year). You will then need your essential notary supplies, (mainly your notary seal) at an average cost of $30. You can spend more depending on how elaborate you want to get. These supplies are readily available on the internet. You may also want to consider purchasing "errors and omissions insurance". If you decide to become a certified signing agent at a later time, the one-time exam costs approximately $130.

Be sure to find out the requirements in your state to become a notary public, as the states vary in their rules and regulations.

****

#5 EBAY – BUYING & SELLING

DESCRIPTION OF THE BUSINESS:

There are many thousands of people now making a living, or making some extra income by buying and selling at online auctions. There are several good online auctions like amazon.com, yahoo.com, bidville.com, and eBay.com, among others. This section deals with eBay, as much success has been reported by people selling at eBay. You are encouraged to check out the other auctions to see which works best for you. On eBay you can sell almost anything that is legal to sell. This ranges from $1 items to automobiles and real estate.

To set up a buying and selling business, you can shop for quality merchandise at a discount price, and then resell it at the online auction. You can also do some spring cleaning of your own unused items, and sell them on eBay. It is best to sell quality new, like new, and gently used items in good working condition. You can find these items at clearance sales, closeout stores, garage sales, and even Goodwill stores. Be sure to see Seller Central & the "What's Hot" list to find out what sells best. You can also do some research on your own by surfing eBay to see if items you have an idea to sell are selling well, and this also gives you a very good idea of what price these items are selling for, as well as the average shipping price. (Also, see the "completed items" on the lower left column of an eBay sales item to see the final selling prices and how many have sold recently). Excellent learning tutorials are available on the eBay website to teach you everything you need to know to succeed.

Success stories have been reported by those selling children's educational items, and brand name toys. Also, videos, books, anything electronic, and home accessories. You can sell almost anything on eBay, since there is someone somewhere in the world (and usually more than one person) who is looking for exactly that item. This is a good place for people looking for something specific at a discount price. Be sure to consider the cost of shipping in items you sell, as very heavy items may be expensive to ship, but you do have the option of stating in you item listing that the item is available for pick-up only. You can state in your ad, as most people do, that shipping is the buyer's expense.

NECESSARY SKILLS & KNOWLEDGE:

Quite simply, you need to have something to sell, and you need to be honest about all the details for every item you list. This will help assure you build a good reputation, and buyers will keep buying from you.

Setting up an account is very simple, and involves filling out an online form. Excellent eBay learning tutorials on the website will teach you absolutely everything you need to know to get started and become successful at selling on eBay. You build a reputation by others leaving feedback about the items they purchase from you, and you can check the reputation of those bidding on your items at any time. You are also allowed to set a reserve price to be sure you get the minimum value for your item. Most people simply start the bidding at the lowest price they will accept instead of using a reserve price auction, unless it is a very expensive item. The fees are also very reasonable, especially for such a huge audience that you can reach (the entire world). The only extra fees are for Paypal, which gives you the added benefits of accepting online credit card purchases and direct bank to bank transfers from the buyers account to yours. These are secured transactions, and are preferable to many experienced eBayers who enjoy the instant payment. These fees are also very reasonable. All of the fees can be reviewed on the online help sections.

AVERAGE EARNINGS:

Earnings are based on the price of the items you sell, and how many hours you put into selling on eBay. This can range from someone who just sells items once in a while for an extra few hundred dollars per year, to the dedicated eBay entrepreneur who is earning $10,000 to $50,000 per year, or more.

START-UP COSTS:

You can start with as little as $1 by purchasing a quality video at a yard sale or the local Goodwill store, and reselling it for $7. You choose what you want to spend to start the business. You could even start with zero, by doing some spring cleaning of your own unused items in your home.

****

#6 EBAY – MAKE & SELL ANYTHING

DESCRIPTION OF THE BUSINESS:

There are many thousands of people now making a living, or making an extra income by selling homemade crafts at online auctions. There are several good online auctions like amazon.com, yahoo.com, bidville.com, and ebay.com, among others. Much success has been reported with people selling at eBay, which may be due to the fact that you can sell almost anything that is legal to sell on eBay, so this section is devoted to the eBay online auction. You are encouraged to see all the auctions and choose the one that is best for you.

What can you make and sell? Anything legal. You can make and sell your own crafts, and even turn your favorite hobby into a business. Examples are: jewelry, candles, paintings, woodworking crafts, and sewing projects. Also knitting and crotchet projects like an afghan, blanket, scarf, or anything else you can think of. Be sure to see Seller Central & the "What's Hot" list to find out what sells best. EBay also has excellent learning tutorials to teach you everything you need to know to succeed.

You simply make your quality merchandise, and then offer it for sale at the online auction. You can also do some research on your own by surfing eBay to see if items you have an idea to sell are selling well, and this also gives you a very good idea of what price these items are selling for, as well as the average shipping price. (Also, see the "completed items" on the lower left column of an eBay sales item to get a good idea of the final selling price and shipping costs, plus how many have sold recently).

Success stories have been reported by those selling hand sewn uniforms, draperies, pillowcases, seasonal tablecloths, items with inscriptions and embroidery, hand knitted or crochet baby items, blankets, seasonal items like Christmas crafts, paintings, and yard display items. If you have a hobby of fixing up automobiles, even those can be sold on eBay. You can sell almost anything under the sun on eBay, as there is someone somewhere in the world (and usually more than one person) who is looking for exactly that item, and this is the best place to find that one exact item they want.

For a little extra income, you can also do some spring cleaning of your own unused items, and sell them on eBay. It is best to sell quality new, like new, and gently used items in good working condition. Be sure to consider the cost of shipping in items you sell, as very heavy items may be expensive to ship, but you do have the option of stating in you item listing that the item is available for pick-up only. You can state in your ad that shipping is at the buyer's expense, which is most often the case.

NECESSARY SKILLS & KNOWLEDGE:

Quite simply, you need to have something to sell, and you need to be honest about all the details for every item you list. This will help assure you build a good reputation, and buyers will keep buying from you.

Setting up an account is very simple, and involves filling out an online form. EBay offers excellent tutorials on their website that will teach you absolutely everything you need to know to get started and become successful at selling on eBay. You build a reputation by others leaving feedback about the items they purchase from you, and you can check the reputation of those bidding on your items at any time. You are also allowed to set a reserve price to be sure you get the minimum value for your item. Most people simply start the bidding at the lowest price they will accept instead of using a reserve price auction, unless it is a very expensive item. The fees are also very reasonable, especially for such a huge audience that you can reach (the entire world). The only extra fees are for Paypal, which gives you the added benefits of accepting online credit card purchases and direct bank to bank transfers from the buyers account to yours. These are secured transactions, and are preferable to many experienced eBayers who enjoy the instant payment. These fees are also very reasonable. All of the fees can be reviewed on the online help sections.

AVERAGE EARNINGS:

Earnings are based on the price of the items you sell and how many hours you put into making your crafts, and selling them on eBay. This can range from someone who just sells items once in a while for an extra few hundred dollars per year, to the dedicated eBay entrepreneur who is earning $10,000 to $50,000 per year, or more.

START-UP COSTS:

You can start with well under $100, depending on the supplies you need to make your crafts. You may already have all the supplies, so you can start for almost nothing.

****

#7 GIFT BASKET BUSINESS

DESCRIPTION OF THE BUSINESS:

This is a great way to earn a living for anyone with creative or artistic skills. Gift baskets are big business these days. People are busier than ever, and turn to gift baskets quite often. Gift baskets are great for all occasions and holidays, since you can tailor make a gift basket to suit any occasion. This is a year round business, but is much busier around any holiday season. Year round you will have birthdays, anniversaries, baby showers, graduations, weddings, and more to keep you busy.

Gift baskets can be tailor made for your customers with wide variety including: chocolates, candies, music CD's, movies, fragrances, elegant bath items, hobby items, or even toys for children. You can also tailor it to the specific requests of the customers. The contents of a gift basket are of endless variety.

You can get a large clientele by direct mail advertising brochures sent to businesses like hotels, hair and nail salons, real estate agencies, and hospital gift shops. You can also sell gift baskets with very low advertising fees on eBay. Be sure to see the section on "eBay Make and Sell Anything". You could even open an online store. You can also advertise in your local paper around holidays. You can also check into exhibiting your gift baskets at craft fairs, home shows, and fund raising events at schools and churches.

NECESSARY SKILLS & KNOWLEDGE:

It helps to have a natural creative flare, or a visual sense of what looks appealing in gift basket design. You have to be able to make your gift baskets look attractive to your customers for new and repeat business. You can get ideas by searching on the internet for gift baskets, and look at the pictures displayed of the many types of gift baskets available. This will also help you find out what the gift baskets are selling for.

AVERAGE EARNINGS:

In the gift basket business you can make anywhere from $5,000 per year for a part-time holiday only business to $50,000 per year or more. It all depends on the price of the gift baskets you sell, how many gift baskets you sell, and the amount of time you want to put into the business.

A gift basket costs anywhere from $10 with simple items to $250 (or more) with expensive champagne or jewelry. The average cost of a gift basket ranges from $30 to $70. You will have to subtract the cost of your supplies to figure your actual income. Remember that all business expenses, including supplies are tax deductible.

START-UP COSTS:

Start-up costs involve your advertising expenses and the supplies for your gift baskets. The start-up costs can run anywhere from $100 to $450 depending on the type of gift baskets you choose to start with.

Your basic supplies include the gift baskets themselves, the decorative outer wrap paper, special shredded paper, ribbons, and the actual gift items. You will earn more if you can obtain the gift basket supplies in bulk, or at a discount price. It is best to not start out with items that will soon expire or wilt, like perishable foods and flowers. If you are unable to sell them immediately, you can lose money. You will also need to make at least a few gift baskets and take pictures of them to display in your advertising material.

****

#8 CPR-BLS INSTRUCTOR

DESCRIPTION OF THE BUSINESS:

CPR stands for cardiopulmonary resuscitation. This is alternately called BLS or basic life support. The requirements to become a CPR-BLS Instructor can vary in different states or with different affiliate organizations (explained later), so be sure to check your local requirements.

Becoming an instructor involves completing the CPR-BLS Instructor course (about 16 hours long, and costs about $125) so that you are allowed to issue CPR-BLS cards to others. You would also want to practice the CPR skills you learn so you can teach it accurately with skill and efficiency. You also need to carefully read all the material in the course until you have a very good understanding of everything involved in CPR.

To find locations offering courses for CPR-BLS instructors, look up "First Aid Instruction", "CPR Instruction", or "BLS Instruction" in your local yellow pages, or on an internet search including your city and state. Also check on the local requirements, and get a complete information packet from locations near you that offer the courses.

Most people who are in the healthcare industry need a CPR-BLS card initiated and renewed every one to two years. This is a huge clientele involving nurses, respiratory therapist, radiology technicians, paramedics, emergency medical technicians, and physician's office staff. Also, most people involved in daycare centers and in-home family daycare providers also have the initial and renewal CPR requirements. Therefore, you can target everyone in healthcare and daycare. To obtain clients, you can contact the daycare licensing office in your area to be placed on their list of CPR providers, and possibly get groups of in-home daycare license applicants in groups as they go through their daycare licensing process. To reach healthcare providers, see about placing ads in hospital newsletters, and direct mail to physicians' offices.

You can also target new moms who want to learn infant CPR as an added protection for their new baby. Check hospitals, and labor and delivery centers. You can also target any medium to large business to advertise CPR training for their employees. Many business owners promote health and safety classes because they are good for the company, the employee, and the community. They may contract with you for yearly or semi-yearly classes for new employees and for refresher courses.

You can provide one-on-one mobile CPR instruction, or have one or more people at your home for classes. Generally, the more people you have attending a single class, the more you can make for that one class. However, some private CPR Instructors in business for themselves enjoy smaller classes and one-on-one instruction. Some participants are willing to pay more for classes scheduled at their convenience in a small group, or singly. Other participants may have missed the CPR class they needed, and must find alternate instruction within a certain time frame in order to keep their license. Some healthcare personnel may have yearly CPR classes given free to all employees by the hospital, but the days and times are not convenient for all the employees. There are many who still use outside services and independent instructors.

You would also need to renew your CPR-BLS instructor certification as required by your state. In some states, this may be simply a matter of performing a certain minimum number of CPR classes in the two year period, such as a minimum of 4 classes; and also you will need to read any new material and changes to CPR methods. Be sure to check the requirements in your state and with your affiliate agency.

You will need to be affiliated with an agency that gives you the certification or credentials of CPR-BLS Instructor, and they are the affiliate agency for any cards you give to your clients. A few of the agencies offering affiliations include the American Safety and Health Institute, the American Heart Association, and the American Red Cross. You may be able to receive the CPR-BLS Instructor course directly from one of these agencies, if they have an office in your area. Otherwise, most communities have alternate affiliate locations that offer the necessary courses.

NECESSARY SKILLS & KNOWLEDGE:

You have to know how to perform CPR on adults, children, and infants. You can learn this by attending the course, studying the material in the CPR manual, and practicing CPR procedures until you become completely confident in your ability. You must be comfortable teaching others. If you choose to teach groups, you must be comfortable speaking in front of an audience. You can get all the information you need about CPR, and all the training supplies and books you will need to teach classes at your local CPR instruction center.

AVERAGE EARNINGS:

When your are giving classes to clients, there are new issue CPR cards and renewal CPR cards. Generally, renewals are only allowed for those that do not allow their current CPR card to expire. The CPR cards are generally good for two years, however, some healthcare institutions set their own rules, and make it mandatory for employees to renew their cards yearly.

For a new issue CPR card, the classes you give are about 6 hours long, and you can charge between $40 and $70 for each participant in the class. The higher rates are for certain geographic areas, and for mobile one-on-one CPR instruction, with you travelling to the participant's home. For example, if you teach a class at your home for 6 new CPR participants, and charge them $55 each, you will earn $330 for that 6-hour class ($55/hour).

For renewals, the classes you give are 4 hours long. You can charge $35 to $60 for a CPR renewal class. The higher pay rates pertain to certain geographic areas, and for mobile one-on-one instruction, with you travelling to the participant's home.

It is good to allow class participants to pick up the CPR training book from you and review it prior to the class. CPR class participants (especially healthcare workers) are generally expected to be somewhat familiar with the material that will be presented in the class. New Mom's, and other participants, however, may be completely unfamiliar with the material and may really appreciate knowing they need to study a little ahead of time, and have the book they need prior to the class. If participants are completely unfamiliar with the material, the class may run longer than expected. At the class, the instructor must explain and demonstrate all the important aspects of CPR. The class participants must then demonstrate CPR on mannequins and pass a CPR test in order to pass your class, and receive the CPR card, or renewal card.

START-UP COSTS:

Start-up costs are under $300. You will need your initial certification class that costs about $125. You will need several CPR books, and an adult mannequin to demonstrate CPR procedures, plus miscellaneous supplies. You can use a lifelike doll to demonstrate infant CPR. Participants can use the adult mannequin to demonstrate pediatric CPR, with instructions to assume the mannequin is a child. The class you must pay for, plus the mannequin, books, and any other materials are tax deductible business expenses.

If you give out CPR books for participants to study ahead of time, it is customary to charge them a deposit, which is refunded by you to them when they return the book at the class. You can also obtain extra books and sell them to any participants who want to purchase them, charging an extra $1 or $2 if you wish, for supplying the book. All of the necessary CPR supplies are easily obtained at your local CPR instruction center, or through your affiliate agency, or online with a search for "CPR, BLS, or first aid supplies". Your other start-up costs involve advertising your business.

****

#9 FIRST AID INSTRUCTOR

DESCRIPTION OF THE BUSINESS:

Being knowledgeable about basic first aid procedures is good for everyone. Accidents happen, and it is wonderful if there is someone nearby who knows first aid and can deal with the immediate emergency while awaiting professional medical help if required. The requirements to become a First Aid Instructor can vary in different states or with different affiliate organizations (explained later), so be sure to check your local requirements.

Becoming first aid instructor involves completing the First Aid Instructor course (about 8 hours long, and costs about $80) so that you are allowed to issue First Aid cards to others. First Aid Instructors are usually also required to complete the CPR-BLS instructor course prior to the first aid instructor course. (See #9 CPR-BLS Instructor). You would also want to practice the first aid skills you learn so you can teach it accurately with skill and efficiency. You also need to carefully read all the material in the course until you have a very good understanding of the material. To find locations offering courses for First Aid Instructors, look up "First Aid Instruction", "CPR Instruction", or "BLS Instruction" in your local yellow pages, or on an internet search including your city and state to find out the requirements. Also be sure to get a complete information packet from places that offer the courses.

Some workers who are in the healthcare industry need a First Aid card renewed every two years. This is a large clientele involving paramedics, emergency medical technicians, and physician's office staff. Also, most people involved in daycare centers and in-home family daycare providers also have the initial and renewal first aid requirement. Therefore, you can target people in healthcare and daycare. To find clients, you can contact the daycare licensing office in your area to be placed on their list of first aid providers, and possibly get groups of in-home daycare license applicants in groups as they go through their daycare licensing process. To reach healthcare providers, see about placing ads in hospital newsletters, and direct mail to physicians' offices.

You can also target new moms who want to learn infant first aid as an added protection for their new baby. Check hospitals, and labor and delivery centers. You can also target any medium to large business to advertise first aid training for their employees. Many business owners promote health and safety classes because they are good for the company, the employee, and the community. They may contract with you for yearly or semi-yearly classes for new employees and for refresher courses.

You can provide one-on-one mobile first aid instruction, or have one or more people at your home for classes. Generally, the more people you have attending a single class, the more you can make for that one class. However, some private First Aid Instructors in business for themselves enjoy smaller classes and one-on-one instruction. Some participants are willing to pay more for classes scheduled at their convenience in a small group, or singly. Other participants may have missed the first aid class they needed, and must find alternate instruction within a certain time frame in order to keep their license.

You would also need to renew your First Aid Instructor certification as required by your state and/or affiliate agency. In some states, this may be simply a matter of performing a certain minimum number of first aid classes in the two year period, such as a minimum of 4 classes; and also you will need to read any new material and changes to first aid methods. Be sure to check the requirements in your state and with your affiliate agency.

You will need to be affiliated with an agency that gives you the certification or credentials of First Aid Instructor, and they are the affiliate agency for any cards you give to your clients. A few of the agencies offering affiliations include the American Safety and Health Institute, the American Heart Association, and the American Red Cross. You may be able to receive the First Aid Instructor course directly from one of these agencies, if they have an office in your area. Otherwise, most communities have affiliate locations that offer the necessary courses.

NECESSARY SKILLS & KNOWLEDGE:

You have to know the procedures for performing first aid for adults, children, and infants. You can learn this by attending the course, studying the material in the first aid manual, viewing any material on video, and practicing first aid procedures until you become completely confident performing and explaining first aid procedures. You must be comfortable teaching others. If you choose to teach groups, you must be comfortable speaking in front of an audience. You can get all the information you need about first aid, and all the training supplies and books you will need to teach classes at your local first aid instruction center.

AVERAGE EARNINGS:

When your are giving classes to clients or participants, there are new issue first aid cards and renewal first aid cards. Generally, renewals are only allowed for those that do not allow their current first aid card to expire. The first aid cards are generally good for two to three years, however, some institutions set their own rules, and can make it mandatory for employees to renew their cards yearly or every two years.

For both new issue first aid cards, and renewals, the classes you give are about 3 hours long, and you can charge between $30 and $50 for each participant in the class. The higher rates are for certain geographic areas, and for mobile one-on-one first aid instruction, with you travelling to the participant's home. For example, if you teach a class at your home for six first aid participants, and charge them $40 each, you will earn $240 for that 3-hour class ($80/hour).

It is good to allow class participants to pick up the first aid training book from you and review it prior to the class. It helps the class participants (especially those who do not work in healthcare) to become somewhat familiar with the material that will be presented in the class. If participants are completely unfamiliar with the material, the class may run longer than expected. At the class, the instructor must explain and demonstrate all the important aspects of first aid, and show a first aid video to the participants. The class participants must then demonstrate their knowledge to the instructor and pass a first aid test in order to pass your class, and receive the first aid card.

START-UP COSTS:

Start-up costs are under $400. You will need your initial certification class that costs about $80, plus the CPR Instructor course that costs about $125, plus miscellaneous supplies. You will need several first aid books and at least one first aid video. All of these costs are tax deductible business expenses.

If you give out first aid books for participants to study ahead of time, it is customary to charge them a deposit, which is refunded by you to them when they return the book at the class. You can also obtain extra books and first aid kits, to sell them to any participants who want to purchase them. Some instructors charge an extra $1 or $2 above cost for supplying these materials. All of the necessary first aid supplies are easily obtained at your local first aid instruction center, or through your affiliate agency, or online with a search for "CPR, BLS, or first aid supplies". Your other start-up costs involve advertising your business.

****

#10 PERSONAL FITNESS TRAINER

DESCRIPTION OF THE BUSINESS:

This is a great business for those who love to exercise, and have made exercise a part of their daily lives. Americans are trying harder than ever to get fit. It gets harder to stay slim as people age and the metabolism slows down, and the mean age of the population is increasing as baby boomers age. This means more people than ever who need to put in more effort in order to attain and maintain their ideal weight and fitness levels. While diet plays a major role, exercise is the second most important thing in weight management and fitness.

Personal fitness trainers design exercise routines for individuals or small groups, and guide the client in their workout at the clients home, their own home, or the gym. You must design the workout plan to fit each individual as in the type of exercise, duration of the exercises, number of routines per week, and hours per week to spend on exercise. You can also give them the basics of healthful, balanced, low calorie dieting, as this will promote weight loss and motivate your clients to keep returning to you.

You can give single or small group classes at your home (after checking zoning laws). Your clients can attend your aerobics classes, or work out on equipment you have, like weight training. It is best to do both aerobic and muscle training exercises for balance.

You can target anyone wanting to lose weight, maintain a certain weight, or gain muscle. You can attempt to establish affiliations with local weight loss organizations like Weight Watchers, and others who teach mainly the nutritional side of losing weight. You can also target pregnant mom's for exercise suited to them, or post pregnancy mom's who want to lose the extra weight gained while carrying a child. Alternately, you could teach yoga.

NECESSARY SKILLS & KNOWLEDGE:

If helps if you already know a lot about exercise and fitness. If not, you would need to spend some time studying these subjects, and actually performing the exercises you plan to recommend to clients. There is a wealth of information on the internet and books on subjects you must be expert at including exercise (aerobic and muscle training), fitness, metabolism, and diet. Also plan to teach your clients the many physical health benefits of performing exercise, including increased energy levels, improved muscle tone, improved figure and physique, lower resting heart rate and blood pressure, keeps you looking younger longer, and may even extend our lives. Beyond weight management, fitness helps

37

to improve mental health, increase self-esteem, and increase overall sense of well being. You must also be fit, as clients will not take you seriously if you are not practicing what you preach.

AVERAGE EARNINGS:

Personal fitness trainers earnings vary widely, but average between $20 and $70 per hour. The higher rates are for certain geographic areas, and high income clientele. In moderate income areas, clients may be more difficult to reach, so fitness trainers in moderate income areas usually work with small groups of 3 to 4 clients. On average, the fitness classes are given for one hour, three times per week. However, some clients may prefer a lot more exercise time, especially in the beginning stages of weight loss while they are highly motivated.

For example, assume you have a group of four clients at your home for a one-hour exercise class, three times per week. The fitness class includes an all over workout with high-impact aerobics, plus weights, and floor exercises. The clients pay weekly, and you can charge each client $10 to $25 per week. Your earning in this example for 3 hours of work range from $40 to $100. You can easily add a second group, or more groups to increase your income, or perform one-on-one fitness training, in combination with small group fitness training.

START-UP COSTS:

Start-up costs can range from well under $100 to $450. If you go to other clients homes, and they have their own exercise equipment, you have very little start up costs. If you go to a gym with your clients, you and they would have to pay for gym membership at $25 to $75 per month. If you have the classes at your home, or you advertise that you supply all needed exercise equipment, you will need to purchase exercise equipment, exercise mats, exercise videos, DVD's CD's, or cassettes, and fitness/exercise/nutrition books. Exercise equipment can include weights, resistance devices, and simple blocks for stepping stairs to get started. You can always add an exercise bike or treadmill later if you so choose, but these items are not essential in every exercise routine. You can start with very little equipment depending on the exercises you plan to use, and purchase more expensive equipment at a later time if you prefer, when your business is a success.

Your other expense is advertising. To reach clients, try to gain affiliations with local weight loss, diet, and nutrition centers in your area that teach only nutrition, and may welcome the partnership with fitness trainers for their clients. You can also advertise in major local newspapers, and in the yellow pages. In newspapers, advertise heavy in January when people are making resolutions to lose weight and get fit. Remember that keeping your clients motivated is the key to your success. They will want to see results, and soon.

****

#11 COMPUTER TUTOR - TRAINER

DESCRIPTION OF THE BUSINESS:

This is a good business for those who have computer savvy. If you know how to easily and accurately use your computer and software, with competence and efficiency you can teach others these skills as a professional computer tutor.

You can target senior citizens who are retired, and have time to learn new hobbies. Many of them have never used a computer and it is a skill they would like to learn. Also, there are some moms who have stayed at home raising young children, and have never had the time to learn how to properly use a computer. They may also want to re-enter the workforce, or newly enter the workforce, and know that almost every job now requires you know the basics of using a computer in order to be considered for any job opening. These two groups of people can be targeted to supply many clients.

One successful home business expert shares her success story. She has targeted only retired persons living at retirement villages and assisted living nursing homes and rehabilitation centers. She teaches groups of 3 people for 1-½ hour sessions and charges them $12 each per session. Therefore she makes $36 for 1-½ hours of work. She has many of these groups of 3 going now, and a waiting list to enable her to work full time, but she chooses to stay part-time. She is her own boss, sets her own hours, and loves teaching others. She chooses the groups of 3 to make more money per hour than individual tutoring, and finds that 3 is the maximum she can teach and give each of them the individualized attention they need. Also 3 is the maximum for all to be able to sit close enough to the computer to see everything being taught. She works three days per week, eight hours per day, at several different retirement living centers. She takes her computer, monitor, and printer and hooks it all up at the retirement center at the beginning of the day. She teaches 1-½ classes, with short breaks in between, with about 4 classes in a day. The total income for the 8 hour day is $144 at $12 per participant, per class. The 8 hours also includes adequate time for disassembling and reassembling the connections on the computer and accessories at the location of the day, and also includes travel time.

You can set up your business in a similar style, or combine small groups with one-on-one classes. You can offer tutoring at your home, a client's home, or an alternate site. You can target retired people by advertising in newsletters and brochures directed at seniors. Direct mail to senior citizen recreations centers, assisted living retirement homes, and to the activity or recreation director or therapist at these locations. You will find some recreation directors who are always looking for new ideas for entertainment and education. You can also place ads in local newspapers, brochures, and newsletters, especially those that target seniors and mothers with children.

Most often, individual clients already own the desktop computer and accessories; they just want to learn how to utilize it more efficiently, and learn new things. Or they may have a specific type of software they want to learn more about.

NECESSARY SKILLS & KNOWLEDGE:

You must know how to navigate a computer and its accessories, and software with skill, competence, and efficiency. You must have a lot of patience for novice computer users, and the willingness to answer questions. You should enjoy teaching others.

You can be a professional computer tutor for specific software training. You can choose from the following list of most requested computer training, or find your own niche in any computer software you are expert at:

- Start up and shut off the computer, monitor, printer, and other accessories
- How to navigate in MS Windows
- How to use MS Works , Word, or other word processor programs
- How to manipulate word processor documents inserting diagrams, pictures, etc
- How to add software programs like picture software for digital cameras
- How to download and manipulate photographs, and make greeting cards
- How to get online and navigate the web
- How to send and receive email
- How to shop and purchase items online
- How to pay bills, and manage investments online
- How to print anything, and change printer settings
- How to scan, copy, and fax

AVERAGE EARNINGS:

Computer tutors and trainers can earn between $10 and $100 per hour. The higher range is for degreed and certified computer professionals teaching business groups, and troubleshooting problems. These same degreed and certified computer experts with many years experience also teach, tutor, and troubleshoot problems for individuals one on one, or pick up a computer with a software problem, fix it, and return it to the customer. They charge between $50 and $80 per hour for this service.

Without a college degree and certification, you can still expect to earn $10 to $30 per hour as a computer tutor. You can specialize in specific computer software operation that you are completely competent and proficient in, or in a broad range of learning. This price range of $10 to $30 per hour will help you get lots of clients to start your business. You can charge more as you gain experience. If you wish, you can later take college courses and seek certification in all types of computer and software problems, and significantly increase your income.

START-UP COSTS:

It is assumed you own a computer and printer. If not, this may not be the right business choice for you. You need to be working on the computer frequently, even daily, to gain knowledge and experience at the skills and tutoring topics frequently requested above. Therefore for those who own the computer, printer, accessories, and some software that you are expert with, or can learn to become expert by practice, your start-up costs are quite low. You can start-up for under $200, with your advertising and new software as needed. You may have some of the software, and frequently requested tutoring items listed above. If so, you are well on your way. You can always purchase more software as requested by clients later, and there is also lots of free software on the internet that can be found by searching for free software or shareware. Remember that all your expenses are tax deductible, and your computer and related accessories are eligible for depreciation allowances by the IRS. See the tax section for more information.

****

#12 WEDDING CONSULTANT - PLANNER

DESCRIPTION OF THE BUSINESS:

Couples planning to get married want to have a perfect wedding. The average age of couples marrying now is older than in the past, and they usually have more income, so they want an elaborate, formal wedding. In the minds of many, the bigger and fancier the wedding, means a more serious commitment to make the marriage last. Others may want a small, intimate wedding. Your services can range from the small to large wedding. Most wedding planners prefer to concentrate on the larger weddings, since the income is usually a percentage of the total cost of the wedding and reception. A beginning wedding planner may choose the smaller weddings to assure they are proficient at planning weddings and receptions and to gain experience for the larger weddings.

Wedding planners make all of the arrangements for the wedding and the reception. They sometimes also help make arrangements for the honeymoon. This involves contacting many businesses including: bakeries, musicians, caterers, photographers, and florists

NECESSARY SKILLS & KNOWLEDGE:

You need to know or learn what is involved in a wedding. It helps if you have planned your own wedding, or helped friends or relatives plan theirs. You need good interpersonal skills and organizational ability to be able to make all of the wedding arrangements with your clients as well as the many people you will hire to make the wedding perfect. Wedding arrangements include: Invitations, floral arrangements, musicians, wedding cake, wedding food and drinks, a good location for the reception with adequate number of seats, wedding decorations, a caterer, a photographer, and a videotaping service. Some couples may want you to also help with planning for the wedding gown and veil, bridesmaids and their gowns, groomsmen, ushers, tuxedos, wedding makeup artist, hair stylist, and the honeymoon.

AVERAGE EARNINGS:

Wedding consultants charge either an hourly rate ranging from $20 to $75 per hour, or a flat fee based on a percentage of the total cost of the wedding and reception. Percentage based rates generally range from 10% to 15%. For example, a $10,000 wedding and reception consultant fee ranges from $1,000 to $1,500.

START-UP COSTS:

Low start-up costs that mainly involve advertising your services. The best places to advertise are in the yellow pages, major local newspapers, in wedding magazines, and by networking with others who provide wedding services such as bakeries, photographers, florists, and musicians. You may get a better start by planning small weddings to gain skill and excellence in your abilities to plan larger wedding. You will also have these to add to your resume.

****

#13 REUNION PLANNER - ORGANIZER

DESCRIPTION OF THE BUSINESS:

Reunion planning is a fairly new type of business with lots of room for competition and opportunity for success. As the mean age of the population is increasing, high school and college reunions are occurring more often than at any other time in history. In order to size up the estimated market in your area, you can count how many high schools and colleges there are within a 50-mile radius of your home. For each high school, there is an average of eight reunions per year. There is the 5-year, 10-year-, 15-year, 20-year, 25-year, 30-year, 40-year, and 50-year reunion. The same goes for any 4-year colleges in your area. There are also family reunions that can be added to your business clientele.

42

As a reunion planner, you distinguish yourself from regular party planners, by your ability to locate people, because the main focus of the event is on the people, and not so much the party. Many of the classmates may have missed one or more reunions, and finding these long lost people are a big part of the business.

NECESSARY SKILLS & KNOWLEDGE:

Reunion planners must be well organized and have the ability to plan small and large reunions. You must be able to locate class members, especially those long lost classmates, in order to succeed, and to differentiate yourself from a regular party & event planner. At reunions, the focus is on the people, not so much the event. It is now easier to find people with internet search engines, but may entail some expenses that you have to figure into your budget. Methods of locating classmates include using internet search engines, telephone directories, by contacting school record keepers, alumni associations, previous employers, voter registration lists, birth and marriage records. Also tracking though friends, neighbors, acquaintances, or enlisting a people finding service. This research can take many months, so reunion planners generally start planning a reunion about one year ahead of the event.

You must be able to make all the necessary arrangements for the event. This includes finding a suitable location for the event, hiring a band or disc jockey, and planning for a caterer, food and beverages, tables, chairs, napkins, decorations, etc. You should also plan to have nametags made for all participants with former and current names, and school photos.

AVERAGE EARNINGS:

Reunion planners generally make their income from the money paid by the attendees. The larger the group of attendees, the more income you can make. Reunion planners charge either a percentage or a set fee per attendee. For example, at a reunion of 200 people, at $5 fee per person, you can make $1000 on that reunion.

START-UP COSTS:

Start-up costs are low at under $200. Your costs mainly involve advertising your business. Once you have a contract to plan a reunion, you can do most of the work at home right up until the event. You can begin collecting fees for the reunion from attendees at any time, and use it to make deposits on the band, and to reserve an event location. To find client, you can send direct mail to the high schools and colleges to advertise your business as a reunion planner. You can also advertise in the local newspaper and online for family reunions as well as high school and college reunions.

****

#14 SECRETARIAL SERVICE

DESCRIPTION OF THE BUSINESS:

Secretarial services include word processing services, typing services and general secretarial services. Many individuals and businesses need documents typed in a specific format using Microsoft Word, MS Works, or Word Perfect. Businesses need help with overflow work and some small businesses may rely on freelance secretarial services instead of hiring office staff, as this may be more cost effective for them than hiring employees. You can choose to specialize in medical or legal work, or you can provide general secretarial services.

There are plenty of freelance opportunities for secretarial, word processing, and typing services, and many can be found with an internet search. You can sign up for a service that regularly posts jobs for a small monthly fee, and some of these jobs accept bids. One example is "elance" at eBay under professional services. Also search for "freelance secretarial, word processing, or typing" to find work from home opportunities. Also check for government bidding opportunities for work contracts. Visit the government home page at www.firstgov.gov.

NECESSARY SKILLS & KNOWLEDGE:

You need to know how to use one of the major word processing software programs like Microsoft Word, MS, Works, or Word Perfect. Most potential job prospects prefer documents prepared in either Microsoft Word or Word Perfect. You must know how to use the software quickly and accurately, with all of the editing and specialized tools in the program, and with spelling and grammar checking for high-quality, error-free documents. You should be able to provide a wide variety of documents, fonts, special formatting, outlining, letterheads, insertion techniques for pictures or diagrams, and etc. You can spend some time familiarizing yourself with one of these programs until you become expert at it if you do not already possess the knowledge. MS Word and WordPerfect provide excellent learning tutorials built right into the programs to teach you everything you need to know.

You should have the skill or learn to type quickly and accurately at a minimum of 60 words per minute. You should be able to pay attention to details, be able to work independently, and provide estimates on job costs.

AVERAGE EARNINGS:

44

Most job prospects want an estimated cost for each job you will complete. Knowing your typing speed, plus having experience helps in job cost estimation. The average income range is $2.50 to $10 per typed page using 8 1/2 x 11 inch paper, containing approximately 2800 characters or 500 words. You can charge by the hour for converting handwritten documents into typed pages, or for material with complex tables and charts. The faster you can type with accuracy the more you can make.

START-UP COSTS:

Low start-up costs ranging from $100 to $300, depending on if you have one of the essential word processing software programs listed or you need to purchase one. Your other main cost is for advertising your business, or paying the monthly fees to be listed on the internet as a freelance secretarial service provider, or to bid on jobs listed on the internet. You could also do direct mail advertising to local businesses for overflow secretarial, word procession, or typing services.

****

#15 RESUME WRITING SERVICE

DESCRIPTION OF THE BUSINESS:

People change careers several times over a working lifetime. They need professional looking resumes in order to be considered by prospective employers. Many people choose to hire a professional resume service to prepare the high quality document they seek.

A resume writer works with the client to develop their resume by organizing the information in a professional, organized, concise format. Resume services also can help prepare the cover letter. It is good to purchase resume writing software so you can prepare top quality documents in a variety of styles. The client can then choose the style they like best. Resume writing software also helps to organize the material in the resume to best match the clients requests and the prospective employers.

The target clientele is university students who will be graduating soon and want to enter the workforce. You can inquire about placing ads on college bulletin boards, or in college newsletters. Another good source of business is mothers with young children who are seeking to enter the workforce for the first time after their children begin kindergarten, or are re-entering the workforce after several years as a homemaker. You can inquire about ads in newsletters at local mom's clubs, and local brochures and newsletters that target mothers and children. Another source of clientele is people in the business community who are changing jobs. These people are best reached by placing ads in your major local newspapers.

NECESSARY SKILLS & KNOWLEDGE:

You should be comfortable interviewing clients and discussing their history as relevant to a resume. You should study sample resumes so you can know what key information to discuss with your client in order to convert the information to a high quality professional resume. These skills can be learned by taking some time to learn and type sample resumes with resume writing software, and looking at the different samples and templates in the program. You should be good at organizing data in a logical and concise manner. You should enjoy paying attention to details and accuracy, as it is very important to not make mistakes on resumes.

AVERAGE EARNINGS:

The average price for a one-page resume ranges from $25 to $100. A two-page resume runs from $30 to $200.

START-UP COSTS:

Start-up costs are low ranging from $100 to $300. This depends on if you have good up-to-date resume writing software, with samples and templates, plus spelling and grammar checking software. If not, Office Depot and Office Max have good software, as well as internet office supply stores. Some very good software is even free on the internet, search for "free software". Your other costs involve advertising your service.

****

#16 TAX PREPARATION

DESCRIPTION OF THE BUSINESS:

This is a seasonal business running from January through April of each year. These are four very busy months, with little or no work the other eight months unless you also branch into bookkeeping, which would give you year round business. Some home business owners combine tax preparation with another seasonal business for year round work.

NECESSARY SKILLS & KNOWLEDGE:

You need to know how to prepare taxes accurately for individuals or businesses you plan to serve. If you have previous experience in tax preparation or bookkeeping, that may be adequate, or you can choose to further your knowledge. You can learn to do tax preparation in a few different ways. H&R Block teaches tax preparation courses around the country every year between September and December. There are also online tax preparation courses and homestudy courses, readily available on the internet. Many areas around the country offer tax preparation seminars given free by the internal revenue service, or at low cost in community education centers. You can further your knowledge of tax preparation by taking time to read tax books and laws, especially those related to the groups of people or businesses you plan to prepare taxes for. Accuracy is important in preparing taxes. As a paid tax preparer your name will be made available as a contact person for the IRS, on every tax return you prepare. In some states, tax preparers are licensed.

After a few years of experience, you can also become an Enrolled Agent, which makes you eligible to represent your clients before the IRS and the tax court. To become an enrolled agent, you must pass a two-day examination that is given by the US Treasury Department. There are tax seminars on line, and in many communities designed to prepare you for this exam. Enrolled Agents can earn more for tax preparation due to their verified tax expertise.

You can target clients with an ad in the local newspapers running from January through April. You can also use direct mail to small business owners. Another method is to send letters to a local tax preparation businesses offering to take their overflow customers.

AVERAGE EARNINGS:

Average earnings are $15 to $50 per hour. Alternately, you could charge a percentage of the amount of the tax return, or a set fee per page of the tax return documents. Most individuals want to know exactly how much you will charge ahead of time, so for preparing simple tax returns for individuals, it is better to have a set percentage fee, or set per page fee. You can best estimate your pricing by calling on local tax preparation companies to find out how much they charge for their services.

START-UP COSTS:

Start-up costs are well under $300, and involve the tax preparation classes mentioned above at zero to $200, plus advertising your business. All of the tax books and forms you need are available free from the IRS at irs.gov. This includes the tax books you need to review to increase your knowledge of taxes, plus all the forms any client will ever need. You may want to purchase tax preparation software, enabling computerized fill-in forms, and add electronic filing to your services. There are many types of tax preparation software available at low cost. The IRS also has many computerized fill-in forms available free, and adds more all the time. It is recommended that you know how to do taxes by hand first, to assure you are knowledgeable about everything you need to know before using tax preparation software. Data entered into these programs are only as accurate as the person entering the data. Be sure to read the section in this book about doing your own taxes to get good ideas about what tax preparation involves. Start-up mainly involves a time commitment on your part learning how to do taxes, and keeping up with the changes in tax laws every year.

****

#17 SELL HEALTH OR DENTAL PLANS

DESCRIPTION OF THE BUSINESS:

There is a good opportunity in the sales of health care and dental care plans to individuals and small businesses. Many people in this country do not have either health or dental insurance, either due to not having a job with these benefits, (unemployed, small business owners, home business owners), or the company they work for may not be able to afford to give employees these benefits.

It is important to differentiate these health and dental care plans from insurance. These plans are not insurance policies. You need a license to sell insurance. You may choose to go that route at a later time, however, this easy start-up guide is all about businesses you can start for under $500, and in order to get a license and sell insurance policies, you would need college level courses, and other requirements that would exceed $500. Here we are targeting the health care plan and dental care plan, not insurance. Some main differences between health care plans and health insurance policies are that the insurance plans are more expensive (either to the employer or to the individual) than the alternative health care plan. The insurance policy also sets an out of pocket limit for policy holders while the health care plans generally do not set any limit. Insurance policies also may provide for copays and percentage based fees, such as 80/20, while health care plans do not. One good side of the health and dental care plans is that they do not usually have a waiting period, while insurance policies do. Also dental plans do not have a cap on the amount they pay per year. Most dental insurance policies cap the insurance companies spending to $1,000 per year per participant.

Health care plans and dental care plans are good money-saving alternative options for those who are not currently covered by an employer plan, or are uninsured for any reason. Plan participants can save hundred, even thousands of dollars per year. The care plans give discounts to the plan participants ranging from 10% to 80% on health care and dental services. Some services may even be free to participants, such as dental cleanings, dental x-rays, and exams. Some of these care plans also give options of purchasing one or more types of care plans to include: Health, dental, vision, and chiropractic care plans. There are

48

usually certain doctors, dentists, hospitals, and other plan providers that must be utilized in order for participants to save money under the plans. This is also true of most insurance policies, where you must choose and use certain providers in order to be covered under the plan. All in all, these care plans are much better than not having any insurance at all.

One care plan on the internet with success reported from home business owners selling the plan is Care Entrée. There are also more that can be found using an internet search for "health care plan, dental plan, and vision care".

NECESSARY SKILLS & KNOWLEDGE:

It helps to have some sales ability, but as long as you are a people oriented person, you can succeed at this business. You must have good reading ability, so that you can decipher the contracts of the company and make accurate representations to prospective clients. You will need to take some time to carefully read all the large and small details in the contracts, because prospective clients will have lots of questions for you to answer.

AVERAGE EARNINGS:

Your income depends mainly on the number of clients you sign onto the care plans. This also involves a time commitment on your part, learning the business, and selling the care plans. People can make it a part time business making a few thousand dollars extra per year, or a full time business with income of $45,000 per year. You are usually paid according to the number of clients you can sign onto the plan. Additional income comes from bonuses, and monthly commissions that keep coming in for all participants you have signed up under the plan for as long as they pay their monthly fees.

START-UP COSTS:

Start-up costs are well under $300. Your main costs are advertising, and any types of sales consultant start-up guides, brochures, and other materials you will need from the company you sell for. They may also have monthly dues you have to pay in order to be a sales consultant for them, but in return, many of them have some type of national advertising and name recognition that will send prospective customers your way.

****

#18 PET SITTING SERVICE

DESCRIPTION OF THE BUSINESS:

There is no doubt about it, many people have pets, and we love our pets. Over 45% of households own one or more pets. The most popular pets are dogs, cats, and fish. Whenever pet owners are going to be away from home for a day or more (for travel, vacation, etc), they need someone to care for their pets. Some pet owners have friends or family to care for their pets while they are away, while others take their pets to a veterinary clinic with boarding. Most pets fare better when they are allowed to stay in their home environment due to less stress factors. Whenever the pet owner chooses to allow their pets to remain at home but does not have friends or family available to care for their pets, the pet sitting service comes in.

Pet sitters feed and care for pets. This includes giving the pets some time, care, and attention. Also feeding the pets, changing water bowls, cleaning litter boxes, walking the dogs, and sometimes administering medication. Most also include additional services to their clients such as watering plants, bringing in the mail and newspapers, opening and closing blinds, and turning lights on and off to make the house look occupied. Most also include taking out the garbage cans for trash pickup day. Some pet sitters provide boarding services to pet owners, bringing the pets into their own home. You can also offer pet transportation services to increase your business. Some pet owners may not be able to get off work, or may not own a vehicle to take their pets to the vet for their annual visits, and may need pet transportation services.

You must love animals and know how to care for them, especially cats, dogs, and fish. Pet owners want to see someone who has a genuine love for animals and can quickly make friends with their pets. You must be trustworthy, as you will be caring for loved pets, and you may be entering peoples homes while they are not home. You should be able to work independently, as you will usually be alone while performing your services.

Your primary client base is people who travel frequently or for extended periods of time, and new residents in the community who do not have friends or family in the area. You can target these people by contacting the welcome wagon service, the local chamber of congress, and local travel agencies. Ask about placing an ad in their newsletters, or including one of your brochures in the packets they send to residents. Be sure to leave business cards and informational brochures with clients since they will be excellent resource of repeat business, along with giving your information to their friends. You can also ask local veterinary clinics if you can leave some cards and brochures there for your pet sitting service, and let them know if you are available for their overflow boarding needs.

NECESSARY SKILLS & KNOWLEDGE:

You must know how to care for pets, especially the pets you will advertise to care for in this business. If you now have pets, or previously owned and cared for pets, and you love animals, you will do well in this business. You should enjoy helping others, and be able to perform all the tasks mentioned above in the "description of the business". Work experience at a veterinary clinic is a big plus, but not essential. You must have reliable transportation.

AVERAGE EARNINGS:

You can expect to earn between $10 and $30 per visit that can range in time between fifteen minutes and one hour. Most pet sitters provide one or two visits per day, and offer a percentage discount of 10% to 40% off the second visit. Some have a certain price for the first pet plus $4 to $8 for each additional pet. Some charge extra for walking dogs based on the length of walking time the pet owner requests. Be sure to call local pet sitters to see what they charge for services. This will help you set competitive prices.

START-UP COSTS:

Low start up costs at under $200. The start-up costs mainly involve organizing your business plan and producing brochures and business cards to advertise and promote your business. You may need a pet carrier or two if you provide pet transportation services and the pet owner does not have these. Your clients generally provide everything else including pet supplies, food, cat litter, etc. If you provide pet boarding at your home, you can negotiate if you or the client supplies the food, supplies, etc. You would also need a pet boarding area in your home. You are ready to start anytime as long as you know how to provide the pet care you advertise.

****

#19 RESIDENTIAL CLEANING SERVICE

DESCRIPTION OF THE BUSINESS:

Many people are now busier than ever before. This is especially true of parents with young children who work full time. Working 40 hours a week or more, plus taking care of the children, and taking care of the daily household tasks and the yard work, there is often little time or desire left for cleaning the house. The residential cleaning service is in huge demand and the clientele run from the very rich to the lower income households. For example, a single working parent who has precious little time left for relaxation or fun with the kids, may not make much money, but will still pay a cleaning service twice a month just to get a break.
You will have a wide client base, and will be easily able to find as much work as you want in most areas of the country if you consistently do a good job and develop a good reputation.

NECESSARY SKILLS & KNOWLEDGE:

You must know how to clean a house well, and it helps if you enjoy cleaning. Cleaning is also a task that is easily learned. You should know or do research to find out the best cleaning products for each type of cleaning job, and all the different surfaces you will be cleaning. Some in this business enjoy the idea of getting lots of exercise on the job. You must enjoy physically demanding work to be happy in this job.

If you have supervisory skills, or feel you would like to become a supervisor, you could have others working for you doing the cleaning jobs, while you run the business, set the appointments, assure quality work is done, and set up appointments with new prospective clients. You would then earn your income by collecting the payments from clients, and keeping a percentage of the income for yourself that has been agreed upon between you and your cleaning staff. It is easier to use independent contractors than employees as they will be responsible for their own taxes. See the tax section for more information.

As an option, you could specialize and only perform certain cleaning tasks. This includes: windows and blinds, or carpet vacuuming and shampoo, or cleaning only hardwood floors.

It is good to set up clients on a schedule such as weekly, or biweekly, but keep the option open for one time clients, as this service is needed, and they will frequently call you again if you perform quality cleaning services.

AVERAGE EARNINGS:

The average income is $10 to $25 per hour. Most often you will need to give an estimate for cleaning the entire home based on square footage of the home, and a list of the services you will provide. For example, a 2-½ hour detailed cleaning of a 1200 square foot house including vacuuming, dusting, sweeping, mopping, cleaning 2 bathrooms, and the kitchen for $30 to $50. You should state in your contract exactly what tasks you will, and will not perform.

START-UP COSTS:

Low start up costs between $100 and $300. You will need the appropriate cleaning equipment and supplies. You need a good vacuum cleaner. You will also need a carpet shampoo machine if you advertise this service. You can rent these at many grocery stores. You can find good cleaning products at discount prices at cleaning and janitorial supply stores.

****

#20 POOL CLEANING - MAINTENANCE SERVICE

DESCRIPTION OF THE BUSINESS:

Pool cleaning and maintenance services can be a home-based business with most of the work done at the client's homes. This business is best suited to those who have experience taking care of their own pool, or have worked for a pool maintenance company. Many clients who own swimming pools choose to pay for cleaning and maintenance service, rather than do the work themselves. There are also many who never learned how to take care of the pool themselves by choice, or it may be their first home with a pool.

This is a seasonal business with the majority of the work occurring in the warm swimming season. There is also some year round maintenance to be done on pools, but maintenance needs are minimal in the off season for most pool owners. If you live in a geographic area with a warmer climate, you will have more business over the period of a year than those living in colder climates. Many people choose to close their pools during the cold season, and need minimal maintenance done during this off-season. If you live in the North with a very cold climate and short swimming season, you will have very little to do for about nine months, from September 1st to June 1st. When the pool is open for swimming, there is much more maintenance required.

During the non-swimming season, pool service is usually performed once a month, but this can vary based on climate. During swimming season, the pool is usually serviced weekly. For simplicity, when starting the business, you can offer the basic cleaning and maintenance service only, and make it clear you do not offer any repair service. It would take a lot more skill to be able to troubleshoot problems, and perform swimming pool repairs like repairing a motor, replacing a filtering system, locating and repairing a leak, or other major repairs.

NECESSARY SKILLS & KNOWLEDGE:

You must know how, or must learn how to clean and maintain a swimming pool in excellent condition. You have to know which chemicals to use in the proper amounts. If you are not an expert at taking care of pools, you can consider working for a pool cleaning company for a few months, or until you feel comfortable in the business. You must learn all the basics of pool cleaning and maintenance.

You should also get books for review and for reference. There are books about cleaning and maintaining pools that you can study independently. There are brochures available free or reasonably priced at many swimming pool supply stores. You can also purchase pool cleaning and maintenance books at a bookstore. Many of these books and pool care guides will tell you everything you need to know about the chemicals, how much to add, when to add them, cleaning products, metal control products, filter products, and spa cleaning and maintenance. You also need to know how to calculate the size of the pool and gallons of water in the pool, in order to add the right amount of chemicals. There are many chemicals to learn about in addition to chlorine. You have to be able to check for balance in the pool chemicals.

You need to know how to use regular cleaning tools and specialized cleaning tools. You also have to know basic operation of the motor, filter, and valves, which are best learned by experience. All swimming pools must be cleaned properly, on a regular schedule. People want to see their swimming pools look clean and sparkling blue, so you have to know how to get it that way, and keep it that way.

AVERAGE EARNINGS:

The earnings vary greatly depending on the climate where you live, with higher yearly income in warmer climates. For your best estimate, call around in your area to see what other pool cleaning companies are charging, and what they include. Most often, they charge a per visit fee, or a monthly fee that includes all of the regular chemicals and cleaning needs. An average per visit fee ranges from $25 to $50 and includes the chlorine, plus checking for chemical balance, cleaning out debris, adding filtration supplies if needed, and brushing the pool walls as needed. The average maintenance visit for a regular customer takes about ½ hour to one hour. Extra charges would be for specialized cleaning and maintenance needs. Some customers may only want an occasional visit, such as to clean and vacuum the entire pool, and perform basic water analysis testing. You can have a separate fee for this service which averages $70 and takes about one to two hours.

START-UP COSTS:

Start-up costs range from $100 to $450, depending on if you already have the tools needed to clean pools. You will need a few different types and sizes of pool brushes, pool cleaning nets, and a vacuum hose. These are your long-term supplies and will cost about $150. You also need water analysis testing kits, chlorine, stabilizer, and some of the basic chemicals and cleaning chemicals that pools frequently need. These supplies will have to be replaced as you use them up. You can purchase enough to start the business and take care of several new customers for about $140. You need to have a pool supply store within driving distance, and it helps if you can negotiate a discount on pool supplies, since you will be buying from them in bulk quantities. Later you can add more supplies and equipment to your inventory as business increases.

****

NOTES

NOTES

NOTES

NOTES

Home Business Taxes

Some home business owners do their own taxes, while others hire tax professionals. This is something you can decide for yourself, but either way, it is good to understand taxes as related to you, your money, and your business. This guide serves as an informational source for learning about home business taxes, and learning about the tax deductions and depreciation allowances you will enjoy in your home business. You can save hundreds of dollars per year by preparing your own taxes, but you must carefully read all the applicable tax guides to assure you are doing them properly.

This tax guide pertains to federal taxes. If your state has state income tax, you can order the tax books and forms directly from your state. This guide lists the federal tax books you will need in order to learn all about your home business taxes, deductions, and depreciation allowances. You may want to start ordering and/or downloading these tax books now and reading them whenever you have the time. Tax books, forms, publications, and instructions are available **free** from the U.S. Internal Revenue Service (IRS). The IRS gives very comprehensive and detailed instructions for filling out all the tax forms. All of these forms can be downloaded from the government website. You can also choose to use their online fill-in forms.

The IRS internet address is:

www.irs.gov

You then choose "Forms and Publications".
Next, choose "Forms and Publications by number".

Then you simply select and download the necessary forms and instructions. You can also call the IRS at their toll free number to order forms, publications, and instructions for free. Most home business owners choose to have a hard copy of all applicable tax forms and corresponding publications or instruction booklets on hand for reference.

The IRS phone number to order forms and instructions is:

1-800-TAX-FORM

The following is a list of the tax forms and publications needed to start any of the home businesses in this book. Also see the IRS samples of several of these tax forms at the end of this section.

Form 1040   - Business income is included here (Line 12 - 2003 tax form).
Schedule C   - Used to calculate your business income and expenses.
Schedule SE - Used to calculate your self employment tax.
Form 4562   - Used to report depreciation on your home, car, & misc.
Form 8829   - Used to report home business expenses.

The following is a list of instruction booklets you need that correspond with the appropriate forms above.

Form 1040 Instructions.
Schedule C Instructions.
Publication 533 – Gives instructions for schedule SE. Self Employment Tax.
Publication 946 – Gives instructions for form 4562. How to Depreciate Property.
Publication 587 – Gives instructions for form 8829. Business Use of the Home.
Publication 463 - Gives information about: Travel... and Car Expenses.

**Note: The only exception to the above list is if you choose to enter the real estate business. For rental income you need schedule E and publication 527. You report your business income on schedule E instead of on schedule C. There are also special forms to report sales of real estate and business property. This includes schedule 4797 and schedule D. You do not need schedule E or form 527 for any other of these businesses in this book as a sole proprietor without employees or partners.

Other very helpful tax books and forms for the home business owner include:

Business related tax books:

Publication 334 - Tax Guide for Small Business
Publication 535 - Business Expenses
Publication 560 - SEP IRA
Publication 509 - Tax Calendars
Form 1040-ES - Estimated Taxes

Personal and business related tax books:

Schedule 1040, form A, B, and D.
Publication 17 - Your Federal Income Tax
Publication 502 - Medical & Dental Expenses
Publication 503 - Child & Dependent Care Expenses (with form 2441)
Publication 529 - Miscellaneous Deductions.

Our government wants you, the small business entrepreneur to succeed since small businesses are the backbone of the economy. The IRS allows numerous tax deductions and depreciation allowances for small businesses. The publications listed above will give you all the information about the these 100% legal, legitimate, allowable tax deductions and depreciation allowances you will enjoy in your home business. What it means to you, is you get to keep more of the income earned in your business. Expert home business owners have found that the "take home pay" for the self employed is usually higher than the take home pay of employees working for someone else. Your home and possibly your car receive depreciation deductions when you operate a home business. These deductions result in very significant reduction of the taxes you need to pay. Your home, computer, office furniture, car, etc. do decline in value over time, however the allowable depreciation deductions are still very generous.

Your home office provides a tax deduction in the form of depreciation. A portion of your utilities are also tax deductible, based on the square footage of your office or workspace compared to the total square footage of your home. Office supplies, computer, printer, monitor, equipment, paper for your printer, printer ink cartridges, all of the furniture used in your business, are only a few of the many things depreciable and deductible on taxes. Read all about it in the tax books listed above.

Business use of your car is tax deductible, if you choose one of the businesses where you travel to someone's home. For example, if you travel to two clients homes for a total of 50 miles one day, you will receive an additional $18.50 back on your taxes as car expense reimbursement for that day, (sample at 37 cents per mile, and increases almost every year). Be sure to keep a record of your miles traveled and destinations.

If you purchase your own health insurance, be sure to read about the self-employed health insurance deduction, and deduct it on form 1040 if applicable to you. Your health insurance premiums may be 100% deductible.

Be sure to note that when your income starts to increase, you may need to make quarterly income tax payments to the IRS. This is due to the fact that there is not an employer taking taxes out of your paycheck. You need to calculate and pay your own taxes quarterly once your income reaches a certain level. This gets easier to estimate as time goes by. See form 1040-ES for complete information.

If you want to have others working for you, it is easiest to start by hiring independent contractors. That way they are responsible for their own taxes. If you pay anyone over a certain amount, currently $400 or more, you will have to supply them and the IRS with a form 1099 Misc to report your payments to them. Be sure to check current tax laws if you pay any independent contractors. If you hire employees, your taxes will be much more complex, and you will be required to calculate various taxes, take the taxes out of their paychecks, and make regularly scheduled payments of these taxes to the proper agencies. Employees will generally expect benefits like insurance, and paid vacation time. Hiring employees may be an option in the future for some prosperous home business owners, but it is easier to start as a sole proprietor, and use independent contractors as needed, instead of regular employees.

Understanding and doing taxes is simply a matter of devoting some time to reading the appropriate tax books, following the line-by-line instructions and filling out the proper tax forms. The IRS gives complete and detailed instructions for each line of every form. You can also email them or call them for additional help. The numbers are included in most tax books under the help section. The 1040 is one example that includes all the help numbers and internet addresses

Make sure to read the IRS "What's New" every year in the 1040 publication, and in each particular tax book you are using. Even those who hire professional tax preparers should keep up on tax law changes since it concerns you, your income, and your business.

The following pages are samples of IRS tax forms. These are the tax forms necessary for most home businesses in this book.

Wishing you the best of luck, much success, and prosperity in your new home business!

Form **1040**

Department of the Treasury—Internal Revenue Service

U.S. Individual Income Tax Return **2003** (99) IRS Use Only—Do not write or staple in this space.

For the year Jan. 1–Dec. 31, 2003, or other tax year beginning _____, 2003, ending _____, 20___   OMB No. 1545-0074

Label

(See instructions on page 19.)

Use the IRS label. Otherwise, please print or type.

Presidential Election Campaign (See page 19.)

L A B E L H E R E

Your first name and initial | Last name | Your social security number

If a joint return, spouse's first name and initial | Last name | Spouse's social security number

Home address (number and street). If you have a P.O. box, see page 19. | Apt. no.

City, town or post office, state, and ZIP code. If you have a foreign address, see page 19.

▲ **Important!** ▲
You **must** enter your SSN(s) above.

Note. Checking "Yes" will not change your tax or reduce your refund.
Do you, or your spouse if filing a joint return, want $3 to go to this fund? . . . ▶

	You	Spouse
	☐ Yes ☐ No	☐ Yes ☐ No

Filing Status

Check only one box.

1 ☐ Single
2 ☐ Married filing jointly (even if only one had income)
3 ☐ Married filing separately. Enter spouse's SSN above and full name here. ▶
4 ☐ Head of household (with qualifying person). (See page 20.) If the qualifying person is a child but not your dependent, enter this child's name here. ▶
5 ☐ Qualifying widow(er) with dependent child. (See page 20.)

Exemptions

6a ☐ **Yourself.** If your parent (or someone else) can claim you as a dependent on his or her tax return, **do not** check box 6a . . . .

b ☐ **Spouse** . . . .

c **Dependents:**

(1) First name Last name	(2) Dependent's social security number	(3) Dependent's relationship to you	(4) ✓ if qualifying child for child tax credit (see page 21)
			☐
			☐
			☐
			☐
			☐

If more than five dependents, see page 21.

d Total number of exemptions claimed . . . .

No. of boxes checked on 6a and 6b

No. of children on 6c who:
• lived with you
• did not live with you due to divorce or separation (see page 21)

Dependents on 6c not entered above

Add numbers on lines above ▶

Income

Attach Forms W-2 and W-2G here. Also attach Form(s) 1099-R if tax was withheld.

If you did not get a W-2, see page 22.

Enclose, but do not attach, any payment. Also, please use Form 1040-V.

7 Wages, salaries, tips, etc. Attach Form(s) W-2 . . . . | 7 |
8a **Taxable** interest. Attach Schedule B if required . . . . | 8a |
b Tax-exempt interest. **Do not** include on line 8a . . . | 8b |
9a Ordinary dividends. Attach Schedule B if required . . . . | 9a |
b Qualified dividends (see page 23) . . . . | 9b |
10 Taxable refunds, credits, or offsets of state and local income taxes (see page 23) . . | 10 |
11 Alimony received . . . . | 11 |
12 Business income or (loss). Attach Schedule C or C-EZ . . . . | 12 |
13a Capital gain or (loss). Attach Schedule D if required. If not required, check here ▶ ☐ | 13a |
b If box on 13a is checked, enter post-May 5 capital gain distributions | 13b |
14 Other gains or (losses). Attach Form 4797 . . . . | 14 |
15a IRA distributions . . | 15a | b Taxable amount (see page 25) | 15b |
16a Pensions and annuities | 16a | b Taxable amount (see page 25) | 16b |
17 Rental real estate, royalties, partnerships, S corporations, trusts, etc. Attach Schedule E | 17 |
18 Farm income or (loss). Attach Schedule F . . . . | 18 |
19 Unemployment compensation . . . . | 19 |
20a Social security benefits | 20a | b Taxable amount (see page 27) | 20b |
21 Other income. List type and amount (see page 27) .... | 21 |
22 Add the amounts in the far right column for lines 7 through 21. This is your **total income** ▶ | 22 |

Adjusted Gross Income

23 Educator expenses (see page 29) . . . . . | 23 |
24 IRA deduction (see page 29) . . . . . . | 24 |
25 Student loan interest deduction (see page 31) . . | 25 |
26 Tuition and fees deduction (see page 32) . . | 26 |
27 Moving expenses. Attach Form 3903 . . . | 27 |
28 One-half of self-employment tax. Attach Schedule SE | 28 |
29 Self-employed health insurance deduction (see page 33) | 29 |
30 Self-employed SEP, SIMPLE, and qualified plans | 30 |
31 Penalty on early withdrawal of savings . . . | 31 |
32a Alimony paid b Recipient's SSN ▶ | 32a |
33 Add lines 23 through 32a . . . . | 33 |
34 Subtract line 33 from line 22. This is your **adjusted gross income** . . . ▶ | 34 |

For Disclosure, Privacy Act, and Paperwork Reduction Act Notice, see page 77.   Cat. No. 11320B   Form **1040** (2003)

Tax and Credits	35	Amount from line 34 (adjusted gross income)	35	

Standard Deduction for-

- People who checked any box on line 36a or 36b **or** who can be claimed as a dependent, see page 34.
- All others:

Single or Married filing separately, $4,750

Married filing jointly or Qualifying widow(er), $9,500

Head of household, $7,000

	36a	Check if: ⎰ ☐ **You** were born before January 2, 1939, ☐ Blind. ⎱ Total boxes ⎰ ☐ **Spouse** was born before January 2, 1939, ☐ Blind. ⎱ checked ▶ 36a		
	b	If you are married filing separately and your spouse itemizes deductions, or you were a dual-status alien, see page 34 and check here . . . . . ▶ 36b ☐		
	37	**Itemized deductions** (from Schedule A) **or** your **standard deduction** (see left margin) . .	37	
	38	Subtract line 37 from line 35	38	
	39	If line 35 is $104,625 or less, multiply $3,050 by the total number of exemptions claimed on line 6d. If line 35 is over $104,625, see the worksheet on page 35	39	
	40	**Taxable income.** Subtract line 39 from line 38. If line 39 is more than line 38, enter -0-	40	
	41	**Tax** (see page 36). Check if any tax is from: **a** ☐ Form(s) 8814 **b** ☐ Form 4972 . . .	41	
	42	**Alternative minimum tax** (see page 38). Attach Form 6251	42	
	43	Add lines 41 and 42 . . . . ▶	43	
	44	Foreign tax credit. Attach Form 1116 if required	44	
	45	Credit for child and dependent care expenses. Attach Form 2441	45	
	46	Credit for the elderly or the disabled. Attach Schedule R .	46	
	47	Education credits. Attach Form 8863	47	
	48	Retirement savings contributions credit. Attach Form 8880 .	48	
	49	Child tax credit (see page 40)	49	
	50	Adoption credit. Attach Form 8839	50	
	51	Credits from: **a** ☐ Form 8396 **b** ☐ Form 8859 . . .	51	
	52	Other credits. Check applicable box(es): **a** ☐ Form 3800 **b** ☐ Form 8801 **c** ☐ Specify _____	52	
	53	Add lines 44 through 52. These are your **total credits** . . .	53	
	54	Subtract line 53 from line 43. If line 53 is more than line 43, enter -0- . . . . . ▶	54	

Other Taxes	55	Self-employment tax. Attach Schedule SE	55	
	56	Social security and Medicare tax on tip income not reported to employer. Attach Form 4137 . .	56	
	57	Tax on qualified plans, including IRAs, and other tax-favored accounts. Attach Form 5329 if required . .	57	
	58	Advance earned income credit payments from Form(s) W-2	58	
	59	Household employment taxes. Attach Schedule H	59	
	60	Add lines 54 through 59. This is your **total tax** . . . . ▶	60	

Payments	61	Federal income tax withheld from Forms W-2 and 1099 . .	61	
If you have a qualifying child, attach Schedule EIC.	62	2003 estimated tax payments and amount applied from 2002 return	62	
	63	**Earned income credit (EIC)**	63	
	64	Excess social security and tier 1 RRTA tax withheld (see page 56)	64	
	65	Additional child tax credit. Attach Form 8812	65	
	66	Amount paid with request for extension to file (see page 56)	66	
	67	Other payments from: **a** ☐ Form 2439 **b** ☐ Form 4136 **c** ☐ Form 8885 .	67	
	68	Add lines 61 through 67. These are your **total payments** . . . . . . ▶	68	

Refund Direct deposit? See page 56 and fill in 70b, 70c, and 70d.	69	If line 68 is more than line 60, subtract line 60 from line 68. This is the amount you **overpaid** ▶	69	
	70a	Amount of line 69 you want **refunded to you** . . . . ▶	70a	
	▶ b	Routing number ☐☐☐☐☐☐☐☐☐ ▶ **c** Type: ☐ Checking ☐ Savings		
	▶ d	Account number ☐☐☐☐☐☐☐☐☐☐☐☐☐☐☐☐☐		
	71	Amount of line 69 you want **applied to your 2004 estimated tax** ▶	71	

Amount You Owe	72	**Amount you owe.** Subtract line 68 from line 60. For details on how to pay, see page 57 ▶	72	
	73	Estimated tax penalty (see page 58)	73	

Third Party Designee

Do you want to allow another person to discuss this return with the IRS (see page 58)? ☐ **Yes.** Complete the following. ☐ **No**

Designee's name ▶	Phone no. ▶ ( )	Personal identification number (PIN) ▶ ☐☐☐☐☐

Sign Here

Joint return? See page 20. Keep a copy for your records.

Under penalties of perjury, I declare that I have examined this return and accompanying schedules and statements, and to the best of my knowledge and belief, they are true, correct, and complete. Declaration of preparer (other than taxpayer) is based on all information of which preparer has any knowledge.

Your signature	Date	Your occupation	Daytime phone number ( )
Spouse's signature. If a joint return, **both** must sign.	Date	Spouse's occupation	

Paid Preparer's Use Only

Preparer's signature ▶	Date	Check if self-employed ☐	Preparer's SSN or PTIN
Firm's name (or yours if self-employed), address, and ZIP code ▶		EIN	
		Phone no. ( )	

Form **1040** (2003)

SCHEDULE C (Form 1040)

Department of the Treasury
Internal Revenue Service (99)

Profit or Loss From Business

(Sole Proprietorship)

▶ Partnerships, joint ventures, etc., must file Form 1065 or 1065-B.

▶ Attach to Form 1040 or 1041. ▶ See Instructions for Schedule C (Form 1040).

OMB No. 1545-0074

2003

Attachment Sequence No. **09**

Name of proprietor

Social security number (SSN)

A Principal business or profession, including product or service (see page C-2 of the instructions)

B Enter code from pages C-7, 8, & 9
▶

C Business name. If no separate business name, leave blank.

D Employer ID number (EIN), if any

E Business address (including suite or room no.) ▶
City, town or post office, state, and ZIP code

F Accounting method: (1) ☐ Cash (2) ☐ Accrual (3) ☐ Other (specify) ▶

G Did you "materially participate" in the operation of this business during 2003? If "No," see page C-3 for limit on losses . ☐ Yes ☐ No

H If you started or acquired this business during 2003, check here . . . . ▶ ☐

Part I Income

1	Gross receipts or sales. **Caution.** If this income was reported to you on Form W-2 and the "Statutory employee" box on that form was checked, see page C-3 and check here . . . . . . ▶ ☐	**1**	
2	Returns and allowances	**2**	
3	Subtract line 2 from line 1	**3**	
4	Cost of goods sold (from line 42 on page 2)	**4**	
5	**Gross profit.** Subtract line 4 from line 3	**5**	
6	Other income, including Federal and state gasoline or fuel tax credit or refund (see page C-3) . . .	**6**	
7	**Gross income.** Add lines 5 and 6 . . . . ▶	**7**	

Part II Expenses. Enter expenses for business use of your home **only** on line 30.

8	Advertising	**8**		19 Pension and profit-sharing plans	**19**	
9	Car and truck expenses (see page C-3)	**9**		20 Rent or lease (see page C-5):		
10	Commissions and fees . .	**10**		a Vehicles, machinery, and equipment .	**20a**	
11	Contract labor (see page C-4)	**11**		b Other business property . .	**20b**	
12	Depletion	**12**		21 Repairs and maintenance . .	**21**	
13	Depreciation and section 179 expense deduction (not included in Part III) (see page C-4) . .	**13**		22 Supplies (not included in Part III)	**22**	
				23 Taxes and licenses	**23**	
14	Employee benefit programs (other than on line 19) . . .	**14**		24 Travel, meals, and entertainment:		
15	Insurance (other than health) .	**15**		a Travel	**24a**	
16	Interest:			b Meals and entertainment		
a	Mortgage (paid to banks, etc.) .	**16a**		c Enter nondeduct-ible amount in-cluded on line 24b (see page C-5) .		
b	Other	**16b**		d Subtract line 24c from line 24b	**24d**	
17	Legal and professional services	**17**		25 Utilities	**25**	
18	Office expense	**18**		26 Wages (less employment credits) .	**26**	
				27 Other expenses (from line 48 on page 2)	**27**	
28	**Total expenses** before expenses for business use of home. Add lines 8 through 27 in columns . ▶	**28**				

29	Tentative profit (loss). Subtract line 28 from line 7	**29**	
30	Expenses for business use of your home. Attach **Form 8829**	**30**	
31	**Net profit or (loss).** Subtract line 30 from line 29.		
	• If a profit, enter on **Form 1040, line 12,** and **also** on **Schedule SE, line 2** (statutory employees, see page C-6). Estates and trusts, enter on Form 1041, line 3.	**31**	
	• If a loss, you **must** go to line 32.		

32 If you have a loss, check the box that describes your investment in this activity (see page C-6).

• If you checked 32a, enter the loss on **Form 1040, line 12,** and **also** on **Schedule SE, line 2** (statutory employees, see page C-6). Estates and trusts, enter on Form 1041, line 3.

• If you checked 32b, you **must** attach Form 6198.

32a ☐ All investment is at ri
32b ☐ Some investment is n at risk.

For Paperwork Reduction Act Notice, see Form 1040 instructions.   Cat. No. 11334P   Schedule C (Form 1040) 2

| Part III | Cost of Goods Sold (see page C-6) |

33 Method(s) used to value closing inventory: a ☐ Cost   b ☐ Lower of cost or market   c ☐ Other (attach explanation)

34 Was there any change in determining quantities, costs, or valuations between opening and closing inventory? If "Yes," attach explanation . . . . ☐ Yes   ☐ No

35 Inventory at beginning of year. If different from last year's closing inventory, attach explanation . .	35	
36 Purchases less cost of items withdrawn for personal use	36	
37 Cost of labor. Do not include any amounts paid to yourself	37	
38 Materials and supplies	38	
39 Other costs	39	
40 Add lines 35 through 39	40	
41 Inventory at end of year	41	
42 **Cost of goods sold.** Subtract line 41 from line 40. Enter the result here and on page 1, line 4 . .	42	

| Part IV | **Information on Your Vehicle. Complete this part only if you are claiming car or truck expenses on line 9 and are not required to file Form 4562 for this business. See the instructions for line 13 on page C-4 to find out if you must file Form 4562.** |

43 When did you place your vehicle in service for business purposes? (month, day, year) ▶ ..../........../..........

44 Of the total number of miles you drove your vehicle during 2003, enter the number of miles you used your vehicle for:

a Business .... **b** Commuting .... **c** Other ....

45 Do you (or your spouse) have another vehicle available for personal use? . . . . ☐ Yes   ☐ No

46 Was your vehicle available for personal use during off-duty hours? . . . . ☐ Yes   ☐ No

47a Do you have evidence to support your deduction? . . . . ☐ Yes   ☐ No

b If "Yes," is the evidence written? . . . . ☐ Yes   ☐ No

| Part V | **Other Expenses. List below business expenses not included on lines 8–26 or line 30.** |

---		
48 Total other expenses. Enter here and on page 1, line 27	48	

SCHEDULE SE
(Form 1040)

Department of the Treasury
Internal Revenue Service (99)

Self-Employment Tax

▶ **Attach to Form 1040.** ▶ **See Instructions for Schedule SE (Form 1040).**

OMB No. 1545-0074

2003

Attachment
Sequence No. **17**

Name of person with **self-employment** income (as shown on Form 1040)

Social security number of person
with **self-employment** income ▶

Who Must File Schedule SE

You must file Schedule SE if:

- You had net earnings from self-employment from **other than** church employee income (line 4 of Short Schedule SE or line 4c of Long Schedule SE) of $400 or more **or**
- You had church employee income of $108.28 or more. Income from services you performed as a minister or a member of a religious order **is not** church employee income (see page SE-1).

Note. Even if you had a loss or a small amount of income from self-employment, it may be to your benefit to file Schedule SE and use either "optional method" in Part II of Long Schedule SE (see page SE-3).

Exception. If your only self-employment income was from earnings as a minister, member of a religious order, or Christian Science practitioner **and** you filed Form 4361 and received IRS approval not to be taxed on those earnings, **do not** file Schedule SE. Instead, write "Exempt–Form 4361" on Form 1040, line 55.

May I Use Short Schedule SE or Must I Use Long Schedule SE?

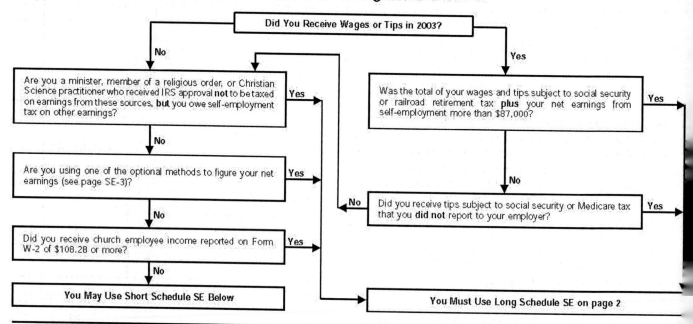

Section A- Short Schedule SE. Caution. Read above to see if you can use Short Schedule SE.

1	Net farm profit or (loss) from Schedule F, line 36, and farm partnerships, Schedule K-1 (Form 1065), line 15a	**1**	
2	Net profit or (loss) from Schedule C, line 31; Schedule C-EZ, line 3; Schedule K-1 (Form 1065), line 15a (other than farming); and Schedule K-1 (Form 1065-B), box 9. Ministers and members of religious orders, see page SE-1 for amounts to report on this line. See page SE-2 for other income to report	**2**	
3	Combine lines 1 and 2	**3**	
4	**Net earnings from self-employment.** Multiply line 3 by 92.35% (.9235). If less than $400, **do not** file this schedule; you do not owe self-employment tax . . . . ▶	**4**	
5	Self-employment tax. If the amount on line 4 is:		
	• $87,000 or less, multiply line 4 by 15.3% (.153). Enter the result here and on **Form 1040, line 55.**	**5**	
	• More than $87,000, multiply line 4 by 2.9% (.029). Then, add $10,788.00 to the result. Enter the total here and on **Form 1040, line 55.**		
6	Deduction for one-half of self-employment tax. Multiply line 5 by 50% (.5). Enter the result here and on **Form 1040, line 28**	**6**	

For Paperwork Reduction Act Notice, see Form 1040 instructions.

Cat. No. 11358Z

Schedule SE (Form 1040) 2

Attachment Sequence No. **17**   Page **2**

| Name of person with **self-employment** income (as shown on Form 1040) | Social security number of person with **self-employment** income ▶ | | |

Section B- Long Schedule SE

Part I Self-Employment Tax

Note. If your only income subject to self-employment tax is **church employee income**, skip lines 1 through 4b. Enter -0- on line 4c and go to line 5a. Income from services you performed as a minister or a member of a religious order **is not** church employee income. See page SE-1.

A If you are a minister, member of a religious order, or Christian Science practitioner **and** you filed Form 4361, but you had $400 or more of **other** net earnings from self-employment, check here and continue with Part I . . . . . ▶ ☐

1 Net farm profit or (loss) from Schedule F, line 36, and farm partnerships, Schedule K-1 (Form 1065), line 15a. **Note.** Skip this line if you use the farm optional method (see page SE-4) . .	**1**		
2 Net profit or (loss) from Schedule C, line 31; Schedule C-EZ, line 3; Schedule K-1 (Form 1065), line 15a (other than farming); and Schedule K-1 (Form 1065-B), box 9. Ministers and members of religious orders, see page SE-1 for amounts to report on this line. See page SE-2 for other income to report. **Note.** Skip this line if you use the nonfarm optional method (see page SE-4)	**2**		
3 Combine lines 1 and 2	**3**		
4a If line 3 is more than zero, multiply line 3 by 92.35% (.9235). Otherwise, enter amount from line 3	**4a**		
b If you elect one or both of the optional methods, enter the total of lines 15 and 17 here . . .	**4b**		
c Combine lines 4a and 4b. If less than $400, **do not** file this schedule; you do not owe self-employment tax. **Exception.** If less than $400 and you had **church employee income,** enter -0- and continue ▶	**4c**		
5a Enter your **church employee income** from Form W-2. See page SE-1 for definition of church employee income	**5a**		
b Multiply line 5a by 92.35% (.9235). If less than $100, enter -0-	**5b**		
6 **Net earnings from self-employment.** Add lines 4c and 5b	**6**		
7 Maximum amount of combined wages and self-employment earnings subject to social security tax or the 6.2% portion of the 7.65% railroad retirement (tier 1) tax for 2003	**7**	87,000	00
8a Total social security wages and tips (total of boxes 3 and 7 on Form(s) W-2) and railroad retirement (tier 1) compensation. If $87,000 or more, skip lines 8b through 10, and go to line 11	**8a**		
b Unreported tips subject to social security tax (from Form 4137, line 9)	**8b**		
c Add lines 8a and 8b	**8c**		
9 Subtract line 8c from line 7. If zero or less, enter -0- here and on line 10 and go to line 11 . ▶	**9**		
10 Multiply the **smaller** of line 6 or line 9 by 12.4% (.124)	**10**		
11 Multiply line 6 by 2.9% (.029)	**11**		
12 **Self-employment tax.** Add lines 10 and 11. Enter here and on **Form 1040, line 55**	**12**		
13 **Deduction for one-half of self-employment tax.** Multiply line 12 by 50% (.5). Enter the result here and on **Form 1040, line 28** . . . . | **13** |			

Part II Optional Methods To Figure Net Earnings (see page SE-3)

Farm Optional Method. You may use this method **only if:** • Your gross farm income[1] was not more than $2,400 **or** • Your net farm profits[2] were less than $1,733.			
14 Maximum income for optional methods	**14**	1,600	00
15 Enter the **smaller** of: two-thirds (⅔) of gross farm income[1] (not less than zero) **or** $1,600. Also include this amount on line 4b above	**15**		
Nonfarm Optional Method. You may use this method **only if:** • Your net nonfarm profits[3] were less than $1,733 and also less than 72.189% of your gross nonfarm income[4] **and** • You had net earnings from self-employment of at least $400 in 2 of the prior 3 years. **Caution.** You may use this method no more than five times.			
16 Subtract line 15 from line 14	**16**		
17 Enter the **smaller** of: two-thirds (⅔) of gross nonfarm income[4] (not less than zero) **or** the amount on line 16. Also include this amount on line 4b above	**17**		

[1] From Sch. F, line 11, and Sch. K-1 (Form 1065), line 15b.
[2] From Sch. F, line 36, and Sch. K-1 (Form 1065), line 15a.
[3] From Sch. C, line 31; Sch. C-EZ, line 3; Sch. K-1 (Form 1065), line 15a; and Sch. K-1 (Form 1065-B), box 9.
[4] From Sch. C, line 7; Sch. C-EZ, line 1; Sch. K-1 (Form 1065), line 15c; and Sch. K-1 (Form 1065-B), box 9.

Form **4562**

Department of the Treasury
Internal Revenue Service

Depreciation and Amortization
(Including Information on Listed Property)

▶ See separate instructions.   ▶ Attach to your tax return.

OMB No. 1545-0172

2003

Attachment
Sequence No. **67**

Name(s) shown on return | Business or activity to which this form relates | Identifying number

Part I — Election To Expense Certain Property Under Section 179
Note: *If you have any listed property, complete Part V before you complete Part I.*

1	Maximum amount. See page 2 of the instructions for a higher limit for certain businesses	**1**	$100,000
2	Total cost of section 179 property placed in service (see page 2 of the instructions)	**2**	
3	Threshold cost of section 179 property before reduction in limitation	**3**	$400,000
4	Reduction in limitation. Subtract line 3 from line 2. If zero or less, enter -0-	**4**	
5	Dollar limitation for tax year. Subtract line 4 from line 1. If zero or less, enter -0-. If married filing separately, see page 2 of the instructions	**5**	

(a) Description of property	(b) Cost (business use only)	(c) Elected cost
6		

7	Listed property. Enter the amount from line 29	**7**	
8	Total elected cost of section 179 property. Add amounts in column (c), lines 6 and 7	**8**	
9	Tentative deduction. Enter the **smaller** of line 5 or line 8	**9**	
10	Carryover of disallowed deduction from line 13 of your 2002 Form 4562	**10**	
11	Business income limitation. Enter the smaller of business income (not less than zero) or line 5 (see instructions)	**11**	
12	Section 179 expense deduction. Add lines 9 and 10, but do not enter more than line 11	**12**	
13	Carryover of disallowed deduction to 2004. Add lines 9 and 10, less line 12 ▶	**13**	

Note: *Do not use Part II or Part III below for listed property. Instead, use Part V.*

Part II — Special Depreciation Allowance and Other Depreciation (Do not include listed property.)

14	Special depreciation allowance for qualified property (other than listed property) placed in service during the tax year (see page 3 of the instructions)	**14**	
15	Property subject to section 168(f)(1) election (see page 4 of the instructions)	**15**	
16	Other depreciation (including ACRS) (see page 4 of the instructions)	**16**	

Part III — MACRS Depreciation (Do not include listed property.) (See page 4 of the instructions.)

Section A

17	MACRS deductions for assets placed in service in tax years beginning before 2003	**17**	
18	If you are electing under section 168(i)(4) to group any assets placed in service during the tax year into one or more general asset accounts, check here ▶ ☐		

Section B- Assets Placed in Service During 2003 Tax Year Using the General Depreciation System

(a) Classification of property	(b) Month and year placed in service	(c) Basis for depreciation (business/investment use only—see instructions)	(d) Recovery period	(e) Convention	(f) Method	(g) Depreciation deduction
19a 3-year property						
b 5-year property						
c 7-year property						
d 10-year property						
e 15-year property						
f 20-year property						
g 25-year property			25 yrs.		S/L	
h Residential rental property			27.5 yrs.	MM	S/L	
			27.5 yrs.	MM	S/L	
i Nonresidential real property			39 yrs.	MM	S/L	
				MM	S/L	

Section C- Assets Placed in Service During 2003 Tax Year Using the Alternative Depreciation System

20a Class life					S/L	
b 12-year			12 yrs.		S/L	
c 40-year			40 yrs.	MM	S/L	

Part IV — Summary (see page 6 of the instructions)

21	Listed property. Enter amount from line 28	**21**	
22	**Total.** Add amounts from line 12, lines 14 through 17, lines 19 and 20 in column (g), and line 21. Enter here and on the appropriate lines of your return. Partnerships and S corporations—see instr.	**22**	
23	For assets shown above and placed in service during the current year, enter the portion of the basis attributable to section 263A costs	**23**	

For Paperwork Reduction Act Notice, see separate instructions.   Cat. No. 12906N   Form **4562** (2

Part V **Listed Property** (Include automobiles, certain other vehicles, cellular telephones, certain computers, and property used for entertainment, recreation, or amusement.)

*Note: For any vehicle for which you are using the standard mileage rate or deducting lease expense, complete **only** 24a, 24b, columns (a) through (c) of Section A, all of Section B, and Section C if applicable.*

Section A– Depreciation and Other Information (Caution: *See page 7 of the instructions for limits for passenger automobiles.*)

24a Do you have evidence to support the business/investment use claimed? ☐ **Yes** ☐ **No** 24b If "Yes," is the evidence written? ☐ **Yes** ☐ **No**

(a) Type of property (list vehicles first)	(b) Date placed in service	(c) Business/ investment use percentage	(d) Cost or other basis	(e) Basis for depreciation (business/investment use only)	(f) Recovery period	(g) Method/ Convention	(h) Depreciation deduction	(i) Elected section 179 cost
25 Special depreciation allowance for qualified listed property placed in service during the tax year and used more than 50% in a qualified business use (see page 6 of the instructions)					25			/////
26 Property used more than 50% in a qualified business use (see page 6 of the instructions):								
		%						
		%						
		%						
27 Property used 50% or less in a qualified business use (see page 6 of the instructions):								/////
		%				S/L –		
		%				S/L –		
		%				S/L –		
28 Add amounts in column (h), lines 25 through 27. Enter here and on line 21, page 1. .						28		/////
29 Add amounts in column (i), line 26. Enter here and on line 7, page 1.							29	

Section B– Information on Use of Vehicles

Complete this section for vehicles used by a sole proprietor, partner, or other "more than 5% owner," or related person.
If you provided vehicles to your employees, first answer the questions in Section C to see if you meet an exception to completing this section for those vehicles.

	(a) Vehicle 1	(b) Vehicle 2	(c) Vehicle 3	(d) Vehicle 4	(e) Vehicle 5	(f) Vehicle 6
30 Total business/investment miles driven during the year (**do not** include commuting miles– see page 2 of the instructions)						
31 Total commuting miles driven during the year						
32 Total other personal (noncommuting) miles driven						
33 Total miles driven during the year. Add lines 30 through 32.						

	Yes	No	Yes	No	Yes	No	Yes	No	Yes	No	Yes	No
34 Was the vehicle available for personal use during off-duty hours?												
35 Was the vehicle used primarily by a more than 5% owner or related person?												
36 Is another vehicle available for personal use?												

Section C– Questions for Employers Who Provide Vehicles for Use by Their Employees

Answer these questions to determine if you meet an exception to completing Section B for vehicles used by employees who are **not** more than 5% owners or related persons (see page 8 of the instructions).

	Yes	No
37 Do you maintain a written policy statement that prohibits all personal use of vehicles, including commuting, by your employees?		
38 Do you maintain a written policy statement that prohibits personal use of vehicles, except commuting, by your employees? See page 8 of the instructions for vehicles used by corporate officers, directors, or 1% or more owners		
39 Do you treat all use of vehicles by employees as personal use?		
40 Do you provide more than five vehicles to your employees, obtain information from your employees about the use of the vehicles, and retain the information received?		
41 Do you meet the requirements concerning qualified automobile demonstration use? (See page 9 of the instructions.) . . .	/////	/////

Note: *If your answer to 37, 38, 39, 40, or 41 is "Yes," do not complete Section B for the covered vehicles.*

Part VI **Amortization**

(a) Description of costs	(b) Date amortization begins	(c) Amortizable amount	(d) Code section	(e) Amortization period or percentage	(f) Amortization for this year
42 Amortization of costs that begins during your 2003 tax year (see page 9 of the instructions):					
43 Amortization of costs that began before your 2003 tax year.				43	
44 **Total.** Add amounts in column (f). See page 9 of the instructions for where to report . . .				44	

Form **8829**	Expenses for Business Use of Your Home	OMB No. 1545-1266

Form **8829**

Department of the Treasury
Internal Revenue Service (99)

► File only with Schedule C (Form 1040). Use a separate Form 8829 for each home you used for business during the year.
► See separate instructions.

2003

Attachment Sequence No. **66**

Name(s) of proprietor(s)

Your social security number

Part I Part of Your Home Used for Business

1	Area used regularly and exclusively for business, regularly for day care, or for storage of inventory or product samples (see instructions)	**1**	
2	Total area of home	**2**	
3	Divide line 1 by line 2. Enter the result as a percentage	**3**	%

- For day-care facilities not used exclusively for business, also complete lines 4-6.
- All others, skip lines 4-6 and enter the amount from line 3 on line 7.

4	Multiply days used for day care during year by hours used per day	**4**		hr.
5	Total hours available for use during the year (365 days × 24 hours) (see instructions)	**5**	8,760	hr.
6	Divide line 4 by line 5. Enter the result as a decimal amount	**6**	.	
7	Business percentage. For day-care facilities not used exclusively for business, multiply line 6 by line 3 (enter the result as a percentage). All others, enter the amount from line 3 ►	**7**		%

Part II Figure Your Allowable Deduction

8	Enter the amount from Schedule C, line 29, **plus** any net gain or (loss) derived from the business use of your home and shown on Schedule D or Form 4797. If more than one place of business, see instructions		**8**	

See instructions for columns **(a)** and **(b)** before completing lines 9-20.

			(a) Direct expenses	**(b)** Indirect expenses	
9	Casualty losses (see instructions)	**9**			
10	Deductible mortgage interest (see instructions)	**10**			
11	Real estate taxes (see instructions)	**11**			
12	Add lines 9, 10, and 11	**12**			
13	Multiply line 12, column (b) by line 7	**13**			
14	Add line 12, column (a) and line 13			**14**	
15	Subtract line 14 from line 8. If zero or less, enter -0-			**15**	
16	Excess mortgage interest (see instructions)	**16**			
17	Insurance	**17**			
18	Repairs and maintenance	**18**			
19	Utilities	**19**			
20	Other expenses (see instructions)	**20**			
21	Add lines 16 through 20	**21**			
22	Multiply line 21, column (b) by line 7	**22**			
23	Carryover of operating expenses from 2002 Form 8829, line 41	**23**			
24	Add line 21 in column (a), line 22, and line 23			**24**	
25	Allowable operating expenses. Enter the **smaller** of line 15 or line 24			**25**	
26	Limit on excess casualty losses and depreciation. Subtract line 25 from line 15			**26**	
27	Excess casualty losses (see instructions)	**27**			
28	Depreciation of your home from Part III below	**28**			
29	Carryover of excess casualty losses and depreciation from 2002 Form 8829, line 42	**29**			
30	Add lines 27 through 29			**30**	
31	Allowable excess casualty losses and depreciation. Enter the **smaller** of line 26 or line 30			**31**	
32	Add lines 14, 25, and 31			**32**	
33	Casualty loss portion, if any, from lines 14 and 31. Carry amount to **Form 4684,** Section B			**33**	
34	Allowable expenses for business use of your home. Subtract line 33 from line 32. Enter here and on Schedule C, line 30. If your home was used for more than one business, see instructions ►			**34**	

Part III Depreciation of Your Home

35	Enter the **smaller** of your home's adjusted basis or its fair market value (see instructions)	**35**	
36	Value of land included on line 35	**36**	
37	Basis of building. Subtract line 36 from line 35	**37**	
38	Business basis of building. Multiply line 37 by line 7	**38**	
39	Depreciation percentage (see instructions)	**39**	
40	Depreciation allowable (see instructions). Multiply line 38 by line 39. Enter here and on line 28 above	**40**	

Part IV Carryover of Unallowed Expenses to 2004

41	Operating expenses. Subtract line 25 from line 24. If less than zero, enter -0-	**41**	
42	Excess casualty losses and depreciation. Subtract line 31 from line 30. If less than zero, enter -0-	**42**	

For Paperwork Reduction Act Notice, see page 4 of separate instructions.   Cat. No. 13232M   Form **8829** (2

OCT 2005

Printed in the United States
35198LVS00003B/109-112